Art Therapy
Exam Secrets
Study Guide

DEAR FUTURE EXAM SUCCESS STORY

First of all, **THANK YOU** for purchasing Mometrix study materials!

Second, congratulations! You are one of the few determined test-takers who are committed to doing whatever it takes to excel on your exam. **You have come to the right place.** We developed these study materials with one goal in mind: to deliver you the information you need in a format that's concise and easy to use.

In addition to optimizing your guide for the content of the test, we've outlined our recommended steps for breaking down the preparation process into small, attainable goals so you can make sure you stay on track.

We've also analyzed the entire test-taking process, identifying the most common pitfalls and showing how you can overcome them and be ready for any curveball the test throws you.

Standardized testing is one of the biggest obstacles on your road to success, which only increases the importance of doing well in the high-pressure, high-stakes environment of test day. Your results on this test could have a significant impact on your future, and this guide provides the information and practical advice to help you achieve your full potential on test day.

Your success is our success

We would love to hear from you! If you would like to share the story of your exam success or if you have any questions or comments in regard to our products, please contact us at **800-673-8175** or **support@mometrix.com**.

Thanks again for your business and we wish you continued success!

Sincerely,
The Mometrix Test Preparation Team

Need more help? Check out our flashcards at:
http://mometrixflashcards.com/ArtTherapy

TABLE OF CONTENTS

Introduction

Thank you for purchasing this resource! You have made the choice to prepare yourself for a test that could have a huge impact on your future, and this guide is designed to help you be fully ready for test day. Obviously, it's important to have a solid understanding of the test material, but you also need to be prepared for the unique environment and stressors of the test, so that you can perform to the best of your abilities.

For this purpose, the first section that appears in this guide is the **Secret Keys**. We've devoted countless hours to meticulously researching what works and what doesn't, and we've boiled down our findings to the five most impactful steps you can take to improve your performance on the test. We start at the beginning with study planning and move through the preparation process, all the way to the testing strategies that will help you get the most out of what you know when you're finally sitting in front of the test.

We recommend that you start preparing for your test as far in advance as possible. However, if you've bought this guide as a last-minute study resource and only have a few days before your test, we recommend that you skip over the first two Secret Keys since they address a long-term study plan.

If you struggle with **test anxiety**, we strongly encourage you to check out our recommendations for how you can overcome it. Test anxiety is a formidable foe, but it can be beaten, and we want to make sure you have the tools you need to defeat it.

Secret Key 1: Plan Big, Study Small

There's a lot riding on your performance. If you want to ace this test, you're going to need to keep your skills sharp and the material fresh in your mind. You need a plan that lets you review everything you need to know while still fitting in your schedule. We'll break this strategy down into three categories.

Information Organization

Start with the information you already have: the official test outline. From this, you can make a complete list of all the concepts you need to cover before the test. Organize these concepts into groups that can be studied together, and create a list of any related vocabulary you need to learn so you can brush up on any difficult terms. You'll want to keep this vocabulary list handy once you actually start studying since you may need to add to it along the way.

Time Management

Once you have your set of study concepts, decide how to spread them out over the time you have left before the test. Break your study plan into small, clear goals so you have a manageable task for each day and know exactly what you're doing. Then just focus on one small step at a time. When you manage your time this way, you don't need to spend hours at a time studying. Studying a small block of content for a short period each day helps you retain information better and avoid stressing over how much you have left to do. You can relax knowing that you have a plan to cover everything in time. In order for this strategy to be effective though, you have to start studying early and stick to your schedule. Avoid the exhaustion and futility that comes from last-minute cramming!

Study Environment

The environment you study in has a big impact on your learning. Studying in a coffee shop, while probably more enjoyable, is not likely to be as fruitful as studying in a quiet room. It's important to keep distractions to a minimum. You're only planning to study for a short block of time, so make the most of it. Don't pause to check your phone or get up to find a snack. It's also important to **avoid multitasking**. Research has consistently shown that multitasking will make your studying dramatically less effective. Your study area should also be comfortable and well-lit so you don't have the distraction of straining your eyes or sitting on an uncomfortable chair.

The time of day you study is also important. You want to be rested and alert. Don't wait until just before bedtime. Study when you'll be most likely to comprehend and remember. Even better, if you know what time of day your test will be, set that time aside for study. That way your brain will be used to working on that subject at that specific time and you'll have a better chance of recalling information.

Finally, it can be helpful to team up with others who are studying for the same test. Your actual studying should be done in as isolated an environment as possible, but the work of organizing the information and setting up the study plan can be divided up. In between study sessions, you can discuss with your teammates the concepts that you're all studying and quiz each other on the details. Just be sure that your teammates are as serious about the test as you are. If you find that your study time is being replaced with social time, you might need to find a new team.

Secret Key 2: Make Your Studying Count

You're devoting a lot of time and effort to preparing for this test, so you want to be absolutely certain it will pay off. This means doing more than just reading the content and hoping you can remember it on test day. It's important to make every minute of study count. There are two main areas you can focus on to make your studying count.

Retention

It doesn't matter how much time you study if you can't remember the material. You need to make sure you are retaining the concepts. To check your retention of the information you're learning, try recalling it at later times with minimal prompting. Try carrying around flashcards and glance at one or two from time to time or ask a friend who's also studying for the test to quiz you.

To enhance your retention, look for ways to put the information into practice so that you can apply it rather than simply recalling it. If you're using the information in practical ways, it will be much easier to remember. Similarly, it helps to solidify a concept in your mind if you're not only reading it to yourself but also explaining it to someone else. Ask a friend to let you teach them about a concept you're a little shaky on (or speak aloud to an imaginary audience if necessary). As you try to summarize, define, give examples, and answer your friend's questions, you'll understand the concepts better and they will stay with you longer. Finally, step back for a big picture view and ask yourself how each piece of information fits with the whole subject. When you link the different concepts together and see them working together as a whole, it's easier to remember the individual components.

Finally, practice showing your work on any multi-step problems, even if you're just studying. Writing out each step you take to solve a problem will help solidify the process in your mind, and you'll be more likely to remember it during the test.

Modality

Modality simply refers to the means or method by which you study. Choosing a study modality that fits your own individual learning style is crucial. No two people learn best in exactly the same way, so it's important to know your strengths and use them to your advantage.

4

For example, if you learn best by visualization, focus on visualizing a concept in your mind and draw an image or a diagram. Try color-coding your notes, illustrating them, or creating symbols that will trigger your mind to recall a learned concept. If you learn best by hearing or discussing information, find a study partner who learns the same way or read aloud to yourself. Think about how to put the information in your own words. Imagine that you are giving a lecture on the topic and record yourself so you can listen to it later.

For any learning style, flashcards can be helpful. Organize the information so you can take advantage of spare moments to review. Underline key words or phrases. Use different colors for different categories. Mnemonic devices (such as creating a short list in which every item starts with the same letter) can also help with retention. Find what works best for you and use it to store the information in your mind most effectively and easily.

5

Secret Key 3: Practice the Right Way

Your success on test day depends not only on how many hours you put into preparing, but also on whether you prepared the right way. It's good to check along the way to see if your studying is paying off. One of the most effective ways to do this is by taking practice tests to evaluate your progress. Practice tests are useful because they show exactly where you need to improve. Every time you take a practice test, pay special attention to these three groups of questions:

- The questions you got wrong
- The questions you had to guess on, even if you guessed right
- The questions you found difficult or slow to work through

This will show you exactly what your weak areas are, and where you need to devote more study time. Ask yourself why each of these questions gave you trouble. Was it because you didn't understand the material? Was it because you didn't remember the vocabulary? Do you need more repetitions on this type of question to build speed and confidence? Dig into those questions and figure out how you can strengthen your weak areas as you go back to review the material.

 Additionally, many practice tests have a section explaining the answer choices. It can be tempting to read the explanation and think that you now have a good understanding of the concept. However, an explanation likely only covers part of the question's broader context. Even if the explanation makes perfect sense, **go back and investigate** every concept related to the question until you're positive you have a thorough understanding.

As you go along, keep in mind that the practice test is just that: practice. Memorizing these questions and answers will not be very helpful on the actual test because it is unlikely to have any of the same exact questions. If you only know the right answers to the sample questions, you won't be prepared for the real thing. **Study the concepts** until you understand them fully, and then you'll be able to answer any question that shows up on the test.

It's important to wait on the practice tests until you're ready. If you take a test on your first day of study, you may be overwhelmed by the amount of material covered and how much you need to learn. Work up to it gradually.

On test day, you'll need to be prepared for answering questions, managing your time, and using the test-taking strategies you've learned. It's a lot to balance, like a mental marathon that will have a big impact on your future. Like training for a marathon, you'll need to start slowly and work your way up. When test day arrives, you'll be ready.

6

Start with the strategies you've read in the first two Secret Keys—plan your course and study in the way that works best for you. If you have time, consider using multiple study resources to get different approaches to the same concepts. It can be helpful to see difficult concepts from more than one angle. Then find a good source for practice tests. Many times, the test website will suggest potential study resources or provide sample tests.

Practice Test Strategy

If you're able to find at least three practice tests, we recommend this strategy:

UNTIMED AND OPEN-BOOK PRACTICE

Take the first test with no time constraints and with your notes and study guide handy. Take your time and focus on applying the strategies you've learned.

TIMED AND OPEN-BOOK PRACTICE

Take the second practice test open-book as well, but set a timer and practice pacing yourself to finish in time.

TIMED AND CLOSED-BOOK PRACTICE

Take any other practice tests as if it were test day. Set a timer and put away your study materials. Sit at a table or desk in a quiet room, imagine yourself at the testing center, and answer questions as quickly and accurately as possible.

Keep repeating timed and closed-book tests on a regular basis until you run out of practice tests or it's time for the actual test. Your mind will be ready for the schedule and stress of test day, and you'll be able to focus on recalling the material you've learned.

Secret Key 4: Pace Yourself

Once you're fully prepared for the material on the test, your biggest challenge on test day will be managing your time. Just knowing that the clock is ticking can make you panic even if you have plenty of time left. Work on pacing yourself so you can build confidence against the time constraints of the exam. Pacing is a difficult skill to master, especially in a high-pressure environment, so **practice is vital**.

Set time expectations for your pace based on how much time is available. For example, if a section has 60 questions and the time limit is 30 minutes, you know you have to average 30 seconds or less per question in order to answer them all. Although 30 seconds is the hard limit, set 25 seconds per question as your goal, so you reserve extra time to spend on harder questions. When you budget extra time for the harder questions, you no longer have any reason to stress when those questions take longer to answer.

Don't let this time expectation distract you from working through the test at a calm, steady pace, but keep it in mind so you don't spend too much time on any one question. Recognize that taking extra time on one question you don't understand may keep you from answering two that you do understand later in the test. If your time limit for a question is up and you're still not sure of the answer, mark it and move on, and come back to it later if the time and the test format allow. If the testing format doesn't allow you to return to earlier questions, just make an educated guess; then put it out of your mind and move on.

On the easier questions, be careful not to rush. It may seem wise to hurry through them so you have more time for the challenging ones, but it's not worth missing one if you know the concept and just didn't take the time to read the question fully. Work efficiently but make sure you understand the question and have looked at all of the answer choices, since more than one may seem right at first.

Even if you're paying attention to the time, you may find yourself a little behind at some point. You should speed up to get back on track, but do so wisely. Don't panic; just take a few seconds less on each question until you're caught up. Don't guess without thinking, but do look through the answer choices and eliminate any you know are wrong. If you can get down to two choices, it is often worthwhile to guess from those. Once you've chosen an answer, move on and don't dwell on any that you skipped or had to hurry through. If a question was taking too long, chances are it was one of the harder ones, so you weren't as likely to get it right anyway.

On the other hand, if you find yourself getting ahead of schedule, it may be beneficial to slow down a little. The more quickly you work, the more likely you are to make a careless mistake that will affect your score. You've budgeted time for each question, so don't be afraid to spend that time. Practice an efficient but careful pace to get the most out of the time you have.

Secret Key 5: Have a Plan for Guessing

When you're taking the test, you may find yourself stuck on a question. Some of the answer choices seem better than others, but you don't see the one answer choice that is obviously correct. What do you do?

The scenario described above is very common, yet most test takers have not effectively prepared for it. Developing and practicing a plan for guessing may be one of the single most effective uses of your time as you get ready for the exam.

In developing your plan for guessing, there are three questions to address:

- When should you start the guessing process?
- How should you narrow down the choices?
- Which answer should you choose?

When to Start the Guessing Process

Unless your plan for guessing is to select C every time (which, despite its merits, is not what we recommend), you need to leave yourself enough time to apply your answer elimination strategies. Since you have a limited amount of time for each question, that means that if you're going to give yourself the best shot at guessing correctly, you have to decide quickly whether or not you will guess.

Of course, the best-case scenario is that you don't have to guess at all, so first, see if you can answer the question based on your knowledge of the subject and basic reasoning skills. Focus on the key words in the question and try to jog your memory of related topics. Give yourself a chance to bring the knowledge to mind, but once you realize that you don't have (or you can't access) the knowledge you need to answer the question, it's time to start the guessing process.

It's almost always better to start the guessing process too early than too late. It only takes a few seconds to remember something and answer the question from knowledge. Carefully eliminating wrong answer choices takes longer. Plus, going through the process of eliminating answer choices can actually help jog your memory.

Summary: Start the guessing process as soon as you decide that you can't answer the question based on your knowledge.

How to Narrow Down the Choices

The next chapter in this book (**Test-Taking Strategies**) includes a wide range of strategies for how to approach questions and how to look for answer choices to eliminate. You will definitely want to read those carefully, practice them, and figure out which ones work best for you. Here though, we're going to address a mindset rather than a particular strategy.

Your odds of guessing an answer correctly depend on how many options you are choosing from.

Number of options left	5	4	3	2	1
Odds of guessing correctly	20%	25%	33%	50%	100%

You can see from this chart just how valuable it is to be able to eliminate incorrect answers and make an educated guess, but there are two things that many test takers do that cause them to miss out on the benefits of guessing:

- Accidentally eliminating the correct answer
- Selecting an answer based on an impression

We'll look at the first one here, and the second one in the next section.

To avoid accidentally eliminating the correct answer, we recommend a thought exercise called **the $5 challenge**. In this challenge, you only eliminate an answer choice from contention if you are willing to bet $5 on it being wrong. Why $5? Five dollars is a small but not insignificant amount of money. It's an amount you could

afford to lose but wouldn't want to throw away. And while losing $5 once might not hurt too much, doing it twenty times will set you back $100. In the same way, each small decision you make—eliminating a choice here, guessing on a question there—won't by itself impact your score very much, but when you put them all together, they can make a big difference. By holding each answer choice elimination decision to a higher standard, you can reduce the risk of accidentally eliminating the correct answer.

The $5 challenge can also be applied in a positive sense: If you are willing to bet $5 that an answer choice *is* correct, go ahead and mark it as correct.

Summary: Only eliminate an answer choice if you are willing to bet $5 that it is wrong.

Which Answer to Choose

You're taking the test. You've run into a hard question and decided you'll have to guess. You've eliminated all the answer choices you're willing to bet $5 on. Now you have to pick an answer. Why do we even need to talk about this? Why can't you just pick whichever one you feel like when the time comes?

The answer to these questions is that if you don't come into the test with a plan, you'll rely on your impression to select an answer choice, and if you do that, you risk falling into a trap. The test writers know that everyone who takes their test will be guessing on some of the questions, so they intentionally write wrong answer choices to seem plausible. You still have to pick an answer though, and if the wrong answer choices are designed to look right, how can you ever be sure that you're not falling for their trap? The best solution we've found to this dilemma is to take the decision out of your hands entirely. Here is the process we recommend:

Once you've eliminated any choices that you are confident (willing to bet $5) are wrong, select the first remaining choice as your answer.

Whether you choose to select the first remaining choice, the second, or the last, the important thing is that you use some preselected standard. Using this approach guarantees that you will not be enticed into selecting an answer choice that looks right, because you are not basing your decision on how the answer choices look.

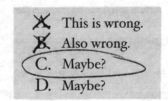

This is not meant to make you question your knowledge. Instead, it is to help you recognize the difference between your knowledge and your impressions. There's a huge difference between thinking an answer is right because of what you know, and thinking an answer is right because it looks or sounds like it should be right.

Summary: To ensure that your selection is appropriately random, make a predetermined selection from among all answer choices you have not eliminated.

Test-Taking Strategies

This section contains a list of test-taking strategies that you may find helpful as you work through the test. By taking what you know and applying logical thought, you can maximize your chances of answering any question correctly!

It is very important to realize that every question is different and every person is different: no single strategy will work on every question, and no single strategy will work for every person. That's why we've included all of them here, so you can try them out and determine which ones work best for different types of questions and which ones work best for you.

Question Strategies

☑ READ CAREFULLY

Read the question and the answer choices carefully. Don't miss the question because you misread the terms. You have plenty of time to read each question thoroughly and make sure you understand what is being asked. Yet a happy medium must be attained, so don't waste too much time. You must read carefully and efficiently.

☑ CONTEXTUAL CLUES

Look for contextual clues. If the question includes a word you are not familiar with, look at the immediate context for some indication of what the word might mean. Contextual clues can often give you all the information you need to decipher the meaning of an unfamiliar word. Even if you can't determine the meaning, you may be able to narrow down the possibilities enough to make a solid guess at the answer to the question.

☑ PREFIXES

If you're having trouble with a word in the question or answer choices, try dissecting it. Take advantage of every clue that the word might include. Prefixes can be a huge help. Usually, they allow you to determine a basic meaning. *Pre-* means before, *post-* means after, *pro-* is positive, *de-* is negative. From prefixes, you can get an idea of the general meaning of the word and try to put it into context.

☑ HEDGE WORDS

Watch out for critical hedge words, such as *likely, may, can, sometimes, often, almost, mostly, usually, generally, rarely,* and *sometimes*. Question writers insert these hedge phrases to cover every possibility. Often an answer choice will be wrong simply because it leaves no room for exception. Be on guard for answer choices that have definitive words such as *exactly* and *always*.

13

⊘ Switchback Words

Stay alert for *switchbacks*. These are the words and phrases frequently used to alert you to shifts in thought. The most common switchback words are *but*, *although*, and *however*. Others include *nevertheless*, *on the other hand*, *even though*, *while*, *in spite of*, *despite*, and *regardless of*. Switchback words are important to catch because they can change the direction of the question or an answer choice.

⊘ Face Value

When in doubt, use common sense. Accept the situation in the problem at face value. Don't read too much into it. These problems will not require you to make wild assumptions. If you have to go beyond creativity and warp time or space in order to have an answer choice fit the question, then you should move on and consider the other answer choices. These are normal problems rooted in reality. The applicable relationship or explanation may not be readily apparent, but it is there for you to figure out. Use your common sense to interpret anything that isn't clear.

Answer Choice Strategies

⊘ Answer Selection

The most thorough way to pick an answer choice is to identify and eliminate wrong answers until only one is left, then confirm it is the correct answer. Sometimes an answer choice may immediately seem right, but be careful. The test writers will usually put more than one reasonable answer choice on each question, so take a second to read all of them and make sure that the other choices are not equally obvious. As long as you have time left, it is better to read every answer choice than to pick the first one that looks right without checking the others.

⊘ Answer Choice Families

An answer choice family consists of two (in rare cases, three) answer choices that are very similar in construction and cannot all be true at the same time. If you see two answer choices that are direct opposites or parallels, one of them is usually the correct answer. For instance, if one answer choice says that quantity x increases and another either says that quantity x decreases (opposite) or says that quantity y increases (parallel), then those answer choices would fall into the same family. An answer choice that doesn't match the construction of the answer choice family is more likely to be incorrect. Most questions will not have answer choice families, but when they do appear, you should be prepared to recognize them.

⊘ Eliminate Answers

Eliminate answer choices as soon as you realize they are wrong, but make sure you consider all possibilities. If you are eliminating answer choices and realize that the last one you are left with is also wrong, don't panic. Start over and consider each choice again. There may be something you missed the first time that you will realize on the second pass.

14

☑ Avoid Fact Traps

Don't be distracted by an answer choice that is factually true but doesn't answer the question. You are looking for the choice that answers the question. Stay focused on what the question is asking for so you don't accidentally pick an answer that is true but incorrect. Always go back to the question and make sure the answer choice you've selected actually answers the question and is not merely a true statement.

☑ Extreme Statements

In general, you should avoid answers that put forth extreme actions as standard practice or proclaim controversial ideas as established fact. An answer choice that states the "process should be used in certain situations, if..." is much more likely to be correct than one that states the "process should be discontinued completely." The first is a calm rational statement and doesn't even make a definitive, uncompromising stance, using a hedge word *if* to provide wiggle room, whereas the second choice is far more extreme.

☑ Benchmark

As you read through the answer choices and you come across one that seems to answer the question well, mentally select that answer choice. This is not your final answer, but it's the one that will help you evaluate the other answer choices. The one that you selected is your benchmark or standard for judging each of the other answer choices. Every other answer choice must be compared to your benchmark. That choice is correct until proven otherwise by another answer choice beating it. If you find a better answer, then that one becomes your new benchmark. Once you've decided that no other choice answers the question as well as your benchmark, you have your final answer.

☑ Predict the Answer

Before you even start looking at the answer choices, it is often best to try to predict the answer. When you come up with the answer on your own, it is easier to avoid distractions and traps because you will know exactly what to look for. The right answer choice is unlikely to be word-for-word what you came up with, but it should be a close match. Even if you are confident that you have the right answer, you should still take the time to read each option before moving on.

General Strategies

☑ Tough Questions

If you are stumped on a problem or it appears too hard or too difficult, don't waste time. Move on! Remember though, if you can quickly check for obviously incorrect answer choices, your chances of guessing correctly are greatly improved. Before you completely give up, at least try to knock out a couple of possible answers. Eliminate what you can and then guess at the remaining answer choices before moving on.

⊘ CHECK YOUR WORK

Since you will probably not know every term listed and the answer to every question, it is important that you get credit for the ones that you do know. Don't miss any questions through careless mistakes. If at all possible, try to take a second to look back over your answer selection and make sure you've selected the correct answer choice and haven't made a costly careless mistake (such as marking an answer choice that you didn't mean to mark). This quick double check should more than pay for itself in caught mistakes for the time it costs.

⊘ PACE YOURSELF

It's easy to be overwhelmed when you're looking at a page full of questions; your mind is confused and full of random thoughts, and the clock is ticking down faster than you would like. Calm down and maintain the pace that you have set for yourself. Especially as you get down to the last few minutes of the test, don't let the small numbers on the clock make you panic. As long as you are on track by monitoring your pace, you are guaranteed to have time for each question.

⊘ DON'T RUSH

It is very easy to make errors when you are in a hurry. Maintaining a fast pace in answering questions is pointless if it makes you miss questions that you would have gotten right otherwise. Test writers like to include distracting information and wrong answers that seem right. Taking a little extra time to avoid careless mistakes can make all the difference in your test score. Find a pace that allows you to be confident in the answers that you select.

⊘ KEEP MOVING

Panicking will not help you pass the test, so do your best to stay calm and keep moving. Taking deep breaths and going through the answer elimination steps you practiced can help to break through a stress barrier and keep your pace.

Final Notes

The combination of a solid foundation of content knowledge and the confidence that comes from practicing your plan for applying that knowledge is the key to maximizing your performance on test day. As your foundation of content knowledge is built up and strengthened, you'll find that the strategies included in this chapter become more and more effective in helping you quickly sift through the distractions and traps of the test to isolate the correct answer.

Now that you're preparing to move forward into the test content chapters of this book, be sure to keep your goal in mind. As you read, think about how you will be able to apply this information on the test. If you've already seen sample questions for the test and you have an idea of the question format and style, try to come up with questions of your own that you can answer based on what you're reading. This will give you valuable practice applying your knowledge in the same ways you can expect to on test day.

Good luck and good studying!

18

Psychological and Psychotherapeutic

JEAN PIAGET

Piaget's identified stages of cognitive development are as follows:

- *Sensorimotor* (birth to approximately age 2)

  One's intelligence is demonstrated via motor activity and initial learning relies on reflexes, such as sucking, crawling, and grasping. Cognitive development progresses from abstract to concrete primarily through trial and error and experimentation.

- *Preoperational* (approximately age 2 to 7)

  One's intelligence is demonstrated via symbols, including those of language, memory, and imagination. Children gain the ability to mentally visualize objects and events and learn via hands-on experiences.

- *Concrete* (approximately age 7 to 11)

  One's intelligence is demonstrated via thought processes that are logical and systematic. Children acquire the mental operations and abilities that afford logical thinking about concrete events or activities, such as mathematical equations.

- *Formal operational* (approximately age 11 and older)

  One's intelligence is demonstrated via symbols logically used to relate to abstract concepts. Adolescents, during this stage, acquire the skills needed to combine and classify objects or items in a more sophisticated manner and perform higher-order reasoning.

HOWARD GARDNER

Howard Gardner believed that intelligence is not a single entity, but that individuals have multiple intelligence that rarely operate in isolation. He viewed intelligence as one's "capacity to solve problems or to fashion products that are valued in one or more cultural setting." All normal individuals possess these intelligences in varying degrees and in different blends or combinations. The intelligences are as follows:

- *Linguistic intelligence* (such as in a poet or wordsmith)
- *Logical-mathematical intelligence* (such as in a scientist or mathematician)
- *Musical intelligence* (such as in a composer or pianist)
- *Spatial intelligence* (such as in an airplane pilot or sculptor)
- *Bodily kinesthetic intelligence* (such as in a dancer or athlete)
- *Interpersonal intelligence (*such as in a teacher or salesman*)*

- *Intrapersonal intelligence* (seen in those with an accurate self-concept)
- *Naturalistic intelligence* (such as in a forest ranger or gardener)

For optimal learning, every individual should be encouraged to use his or her preferred intelligences. Instructional activities and learning assessment should address multiple intelligence forms.

DJ LEVINSON

D. J. Levinson in his 1978 "The Seasons of a Man's Life," provides a definition for life structure as being "the underlying pattern or design of a person's life at any given time." Life structure deals with the way in which an individual connects between themselves and their circumstances as well as what changes and remains stable as one progresses through different relationships, activities physical settings, and roles. Levinson describes it as a sequence of eras, each of which is separated by a pivotal transition time. The suitable life structure for one's age and circumstances is often unsuitable for the next life phase. The transition years serve as a time to reconsider and adapt the previous period, leading to a new life structure.

Levinson's life cycle theory includes the following sequence of events:

- Childhood and adolescent (ages 13-17) - Early adulthood begins in this era as the person starts engaging in adult behavior in the adult world. This era is the one where development occurs most rapidly.
- Early adulthood era (age 17–45)- During this period, the person forms a "Dream" that defines their major goals in life. According to Levinson, the dream gives the individual a sense of purpose and aliveness.
- Middle adulthood era (age 40–65) - During this period, individuals often experience a midlife crisis if they feel their lives will never be able to match their dreams.
- Late adulthood era (age 60 years and older) - This period begins with the late adulthood transition and moves on to concerns of health, retirement, loss of a spouse, etc.

LEVINSON'S LIFE CYCLE THEORY BENEFITS AND LIMITATIONS

Levinson's stage theory goes beyond most theories, in a critical way, by assuming that one's development continues throughout adulthood. The theory is also important because the notion of general stages helps establish pattern of groups and provides a framework to assist with clinical activities. Additionally, periods of stability versus those of transitions is a useful concept.

His theory is limited in application because it was developed by only examining forty middle-class white men, who were hourly workers, novelists, business executives, and academic biologists. This small, all white sample as well as the concept that all people go through predictable life phases harkens some criticism to his theory. Most academic scholars do not follow the categories in Levinson's theory. Many psychologists argue instead that the process of adult development occurs between the individual and their surrounding environment.

ERIK ERIKSON
PSYCHOSOCIAL DEVELOPMENT

Erikson argued that personality develops in a series of different stages and is impacted by social experiences throughout one's entire lifespan. A key element of Erikson's theory revolves around ego identity development, which he defined as being "the conscious sense of self." There are eight distinct stages in Erikson's Theory of Psychosocial Development. Successful progression through a given stage results in a personality that is healthy and affords successful interactions with others. Failing to progress through a stage may have the opposite effects. Erikson identified the eight stages as follows:

- Trust vs. Mistrust - occurs in Infancy (Birth-12 Months of age)
- Autonomy vs. Shame and Doubt -- Occurs in young childhood (1-3 Years of age)
- Initiative vs. Guilt -- Occurs in early Childhood (3-5 years of age)
- Industry vs. Inferiority -- occurs in Middle Childhood (ages 6-10)
- Identity vs. Role Confusion -- occurs during Adolescence (ages 11-18)
- Intimacy vs. Isolation -- occurs in early Adulthood (ages 18-34)
- Generativity vs. Stagnation -- occurs in Middle Adulthood (ages 35-60)
- Ego Integrity vs. Despair -- occurs in Later Adulthood (ages 60 years and older)

DW WINNICOTT
THEORY OF ATTACHMENT

Winnicott's 1951 essay titled "Transitional Objects and Transitional Phenomena" impacted object relations theory, which looks at relationships between different people as well as interpersonal and group experiences. The focus of Winnicott was on the relationship between the mother and her child. During the process where the child starts to separate from the mother, he or she attaches instead to a "transitional object," like a stuffed animal or blanket. Subsequently, the child starts to substitute a familiar but inanimate object to offer comfort during stressful and/or anxiety-provoking times. As development progresses, the child does not continue to need the transitional object. The child's "internal working model" of their environment and world is shaped by these early attachments and they also influence long-term relationships.

SIGMUND FREUD
PSYCHODYNAMIC THEORY

Freud's ideas were that that aspects of the personality develop as one moves through various psychosexual stages, which are each characterized by different sexual gratification demands and ways of satisfying that gratification. If, during the growth process, a person does not attain the correct amount of gratification, then he or she may become fixated in that particular stage and fail to fully develop. Freud thought that much of one's personality is shaped from their childhood experiences.

He also believed that people learn through myths, fairy tales, jokes, folklore, linguistic usage, and poems.

PSYCHOSEXUAL STAGES

According to Freud's model of child development, the human personality develops during childhood in five stages

- Oral stage (First eighteen months of life)
  - Pleasure centers are in the mouth
- Anal phase (From 18 months to 24 months)
  - Focuses in the anal area (their bowel movements)
- Phallic phase (From 24 months to about 48 months)
  - Focus shifts from the anal region to the genital region
- Latency phase (From the end of the phallic stage until puberty)
  - Repression of sexuality which allows the child to develop same sex friendships and to focus on school and athletics
- Genital stage (Starts at puberty)
  - Allows the child to develop opposite sex relationships

To have a fully functional adulthood, the previous stages need to be fully resolved and there needs to be a balance between love and work.

KEY CONCEPTS ATTRIBUTED TO FREUD

In Freud's early theory, he asserted that libido (sexual and instinctual drives) motivate human behaviors. When the urges of the libido are repressed, they are displayed as aggression. He developed the idea of the Oedipus complex as a way to explain the child's unconscious drive for the exclusive love of the opposite sex parent, when they are around 5.5 years old. This desire involves jealousy directed toward the same sex parent and the unconscious desire for that parent to die. During the phallic stage in "normal" development, the Oedipal complex is resolved. If this does not occur, certain neuroses in childhood will ensue.

FIXATION, REGRESSION, AND ARRESTED DEVELOPMENT

Freud argued that each child passes through five stages of psychosexual development. Any trauma experienced during one of the first three stages, a fixation, which is state where a person becomes obsessed with their attachment to another person, animal, or inanimate object, may result. When people are confronted with stressful events, they sometimes abandon their coping strategies and revert to earlier patterns of behavior. Anna Freud named this defense mechanism regression, which is closely related to fixation. The stronger an individual's fixations were on objects early in life, the more likely, when presented with an obstacle in later life, that he or she will act in a regressed manner from an earlier life phase. The concept of fixation exists in other facets of psychoanalytic thought and theory. The fixation-regression system represents one's set of defensive capacities formed during his or her development. Fixation and arrested development are frequently used synonymously.

FREUD'S THEORY OF EGO PSYCHOLOGY

As Freud formed his psychoanalysis approaches, he began focusing on the superego and ego. Therefore, psychoanalysis became, essentially, an "ego psychology." He believed that during the personality development stages, various driving forces develop that play an important role in the way humans interact with their world. According to Freud, humans are born with their id, which wants whatever feels good in that moment, without considering the reality of the given situation. Freud assigned the term "ego" to the second stage of personality development. The Ego's responsibility is to meet the id's needs while considering the reality of the given situation. Freud believed that the superego develops around age five. It is the moral part of the mind that dictates one's belief of what is right and wrong. In a healthy individual, the ego is the strongest of the three forces and must maintain a balance between the Superego and Id.

CONCEPTS OF CONSCIOUS, PRECONSCIOUS AND UNCONSCIOUS

The conscious involves awareness of current perceptions, thoughts, feelings, fantasies, and memories at any particular point in time. It is the element of mental processing that individuals can rationally think and talk about. Preconscious is the memory component not necessarily part of consciousness but that can be easily and readily retrieved and brought into one's awareness. The unconscious refers to the feelings, memories, thoughts, and urges that remain outside of one's conscious awareness. The unconscious mind holds repressed traumatic memories and unacceptable drives that are anxiety-provoking. Unconscious motivations, in a disguised form, are available to consciousness. For example, dreams and slips of the tongue are concealed unconscious content that is not directly confronted. Freud believed these repressed painful memories manifest themselves in psychotic or neurotic behavior and also in dreams. Many recent biopsychological explorations have offered new light on the validity of psychoanalytic beliefs about the unconscious.

ID, EGO, AND SUPEREGO

The concept of the id is that it is the unconscious pool of constantly-active drives that are governed by the pleasure principle. It demands its urges are immediately satisfied, regardless of any undesirable effects. In contrast, the ego operates predominately in conscious and preconscious levels, but also involves some unconscious elements, since both the ego and the superego are thought to evolve from the id. The ego is governed by the reality principle and satisfies the id's urges once adequate circumstances are found. Inappropriate desires are repressed but not satisfied. The superego is only partially conscious, and censors the functions of the ego and comprises the person's ideals that are derived from his family and society's values, as the source of guilt and fear of punishment.

DREAM SYMBOLISM

Freud's dream symbolism musings have imparted much attention to the meaning behind an individual's dreams. He believed that dreams are an important key into one's unconscious mind. Additionally, Freud felt that a dream's events and characters frequently represented one's repressed painful experiences. A key feature of dream interpretation revolves around finding each symbol's referent. To rationalize various symbol-referent connections, Freud drew upon ideas in the law of resemblance. Dream analysis was an integral part of Freud's psychoanalysis advancement. His contemporaries disagreed with Freud's interpretations and his emphasis of the significance of dreams. Nonetheless, works and studies of dream interpretations continue to important to many scholars.

SPEECH AND LANGUAGE

Research demonstrates that most babies, by six months of age, recognize the basic sounds used in their native language. As an infant's speech mechanism (the structures of the tongue, jaw, and lips) and voice develop and mature, he or she can start to produce controlled sound. In the baby's first few months of life, this begins as with "cooing," which is a repetitive, quiet, pleasant vocalization. Usually by approximately six months of age, the infant produces repetitive syllables (such as da, da, da). Around 12 months, most babies can say a few simple words; this vocabular expands to eight to ten words by eighteen months of age. Most children, by age two, can form crude sentences by putting words together like "more juice." During this period of time, children quickly learn that words symbolize different objects, thoughts, and actions. Between the ages of three and five, the child's vocabulary increases rapidly, and he or she starts to master language rules.

Speech disorders may be the result of developmental deficits or delays, neuropathologies, and/or be the product of inherent difficulties in the child or caregiving adult's environment.

- *Aphasia* -- Speech and language ability loss caused by a head injury or stroke.
- *Articulation disorders* – Difficulty with forming and stringing sounds together, typically characterized by improperly substituting one sound for another (such as wabbit for rabbit), omitting a sound (saying han instead of hand) or distorting a sound (pronouncing shlip instead of sip).
- *Delayed language* – A notable slowness in developing the requisite vocabulary and grammar to adequately express and understand thoughts, ideas, and feelings.
- *Echolalia* -- Repetition of simple words or phrases, typically with little or no understanding of their meaning.
- *Mutism* – Absence of speech
- *Perseveration* – Automatically or uncontrollably repeating a particular response (gesture, word, or phrase) even in the absence of stimuli.
- *Stuttering* -- Interruption in the smoothness or flow speech, characterized by abnormal hesitations, sound or syllable (or even word or phrase) repetitions or prolongations.

24

Individuals have two primary, but distinct, separate language knowledge banks.

- *Passive or receptive language* is one's ability to comprehend and make sense of information. It may vocabulary and language concepts knowledge, sequencing information, and short-term memory. Listening and reading employ one's passive vocabulary.
- *Active or expressive language* is a child's vocabulary that he or she uses for speaking or writing. The passive vocabulary of a child forms through constant repetition of words, phrases, or sounds. Once repeated enough, these pieces of language become part of the active vocabulary.

LANGUAGE AND COGNITION

Current beliefs are that language and cognition have complex similarities and differences, but that both develop over one's life from the environmental and cultural learning constraints imposed on one's genetic factors.

PERCEPTUAL-MOTOR SKILLS

An individual's first couple years of life are considered the sensory-motor time of cognitive development. In the process of perceptual-motor development, children learn to move their various body parts as they engage with objects and people. Perception is one's interpretation of what they sense. The first perception channels to develop are typically visual, auditory, kinesthetic, and tactual. Children acquire information through their five senses—what is seen, heard, smelled, tasted, and touched. As children mature, they begin to organize and make sense of perceptions. The perceptions inform motor skills (how to move the body) and responses. Children learn, for example, that ovens through their senses, particularly touch. Their memory of hot ovens reminds them to not touch the oven.

RUDOLF ARNHEIM

Theory of Perception – Arnheim's theories address what it means for someone to "see" and "think." *Visual Thinking,* Arnheim's books, explains the following four different principles of visual thinking:

- *Vision is selective* -- People tend to focus their attention on those elements in their environment that change.
- *Fixation solves a problem* – People can willfully control their visual selectivity such that they can fixate on things that help meet their needs or solve their problems.
- *Discernment in depth* – There is a mutual exclusivity between an object and its context, such that when individuals look at a nearby object, context surrounding it becomes unfocused. When the context is studied instead, the object then becomes unfocused.
- *Shapes are concepts* -- Basic familiar shapes are considered "visual concepts" into which the mind sorts its various experiences with reality.

HAND-EYE COORDINATION

Age-appropriate developmental milestones include the following:

- *Birth to age three* – Vision allowing the baby's eyes to follow slowly moving objects and basic hand-eye skills (reaching, grasping objects, dressing, feeding, etc.) begin to develop. The child begins to recognize place and direction concepts, such as up, down, out, and in, and develops he ability to manipulate objects using fine motor skills.
- *Age three to five* – The child continues to develop skills with hand-eye coordination and a left or right handedness preference. He or she further understands and uses place and direction concepts. Hand-eye-body coordination and depth perception improve, and the child develops climbing, balancing, running, jumping, pushing, pulling, and stair climbing skills.
- *Age five to seven* – The child's fine motor skills, such as pencil and scissor use, improve. He or she continues to develop movement and coordination skills, and learns to focus vision with endurance on school work.

HEINZ KOHUT

The United States' first major psychoanalytic movement that recognized empathy's crucial role in human development and psychoanalytic change was self-psychology, which is a "structural" psychology. Heinz Kohut's concept of one's self structures aided Kohut in developing a theory regarding how and why individuals change between moments, situations, and relationships, and how and why people remain the same, in certain predictable ways. Kohut developed the transferences of mirroring and idealization as part of self-object theory. For children to develop a healthy sense of self, they must be able to idealize admired figures' strengths and receive mirroring (positive reinforcement from caregiving and empathic people in their lives).

OBJECT RELATIONS THEORY

Contemporary object relations theorists assert that people possess an innate drive to create and sustain attachments and relationships with various objects, such as people (father, mother, siblings, etc.) or things that serve as transitional objects (like toys and pets). These various objects and the child's relationship with them get incorporated into the "self", and form the building blocks or foundation of the self-system. One's internalized early childhood self-structure serves as a blueprint or roadmap for the establishment and maintenance of future relationships. As one matures, he or she may form intense or self-destructive relationships with drugs, alcohol, food, other people, or other things. If a young child has traumatic self-objects relations, they will likely be more resistant to change in their later life. For use to bring comfort by children in stressful times, Winnicott introduced familiar objects, transitional objects, and inanimate objects.

DEFENSE MECHANISMS

Defense mechanisms allow people to protect themselves from being aware of impulses that are undesired and feared like unpleasant feelings, thoughts, and desires. Some of the mechanisms that humans use include:

- Displacement involves redirecting impulses, thoughts, and feelings from an undesirable, threatening object to one that is safer and more acceptable. Displacements are often frequently workable and satisfactory mechanisms; if a person cannot have steak, hamburger is likely satisfactory. Displaced anger, such as being angry at one's boss and hitting the dog instead, can cause serious problem's in one's life.
- Projection: attributing one's impulses or thoughts to another individual, for example, an angry spouse may accuse their partner of acting hostile. This defense mechanism is often overused by paranoid people.
- Sublimation: channeling rather unacceptable impulses into outlets that are more acceptable. Sublimation is commonly combined with other defense mechanisms, such as displacement and symbolization.
- Symbolization: an act or object represents a complex group of acts or objects, some of which conflict with or be unacceptable to the ego; for example, a man asks for a woman's hand (in marriage).

TRANSFERENCE AND COUNTERTRANSFERENCE

Transference and countertransference can manifest in all relationships, including those that are personal, professional, and therapeutic. Although its origin is attributable to Freud, transference is the technical term that describes an unconscious transfer of interpersonal situations from one experience taken to another. Transference involves revisiting past relations in currently existing circumstances. Feelings and thoughts about significant others from an individual's past are projected onto other people or a therapist, which, in turn, influence the therapeutic or other relationship.

Transference can inform the therapist about the client's unresolved issues and furthers the relationship's development and the therapeutic process.

Countertransference involves the therapist's response to the patient's transference problems with their own transference issues. During therapy treatment programs, the therapist may develop negative or positive or feelings directed toward the patient, but it is unethical to act on such feelings.

NAUMBURG AND KRAMER

Margaret Naumburg and Edith Kramer's art therapy work were influenced by Freudian theories. Naumburg believed that creating artwork allows the release of unconscious conflicts that otherwise would be later verbalized or too volatile or shameful to share with other people. Artwork serves as a means for insight into control over and mastery of a person's fears. Naumburg began having her patients sketch their dreams and discuss them. She believed drawn images were symbolic communication forms, and as such, she oriented her approach toward the meaning behind the final artwork. Naumburg is, essentially, the founder of United States art therapy.

Edith Kramer's work addressed the creative process evoked in unconscious conflict expression. She felt the art therapist should focus on the patient's psychological situation, the relationships in the art work's formal elements, and its creation story.

Both Naumburg and Kramer's work heavily relied on Freudian theories. To Naumburg, art, like dreams, was a type of unconscious-produced symbolic speech to be generated in a spontaneous way and understood using free association. Art was considered a "royal road" to discover unconscious symbolic contents, both for diagnostic and therapeutic purposes, necessitating insight, verbalization, and expression.

To Kramer, art was considered a "royal road" to sublimation, a means of integrating impulses and conflicting feelings and in an aesthetically satisfying way, to help the ego manage, synthesize, and control through the creative process itself. Kramer felt that the art production process and creativity help one heal. She emphasized that the produced art, as a therapeutic intervention, produces sublimation.

CARL JUNG

Carl Jung, one of Freud's close friends and disciples, shared many similar dream interpretation beliefs. He lost favor with both Freud and the psychoanalytical community at large when he argued that every person shares "common themes, symbols, and ideas" that cover ideas such as love, work, family, or general life. He identified this shared "collective conscious" among all humankind as archetypes. Jung also argued for the existence of a shadow in one's dreams, which represents the person's subliminal desires. Other characters Jung argued commonly appeared in dreams include the wise old man, the gangster, the divine child, the animus, and the anima.

Jungian concepts of the "collective conscious" and archetypes -- Jungian psychotherapy explores avenues of the unconscious mind through dreams, archetypes, myths, spirituality, and the creative imagination. Jung felt that the mind can be divided into conscious and unconscious parts. The unconscious part, he believed, was made up of the following layers:

- Personal unconscious -- An individual's own unique memories and experiences
- Collective unconscious -- shared memories and tendencies that are inherited.

Jung developed the concept of archetypal symbols that serve as the collective unconscious' vehicle of expression. The archetypes are manifest personally, more primitively, in dreams and more complex culturally in symbols, fairy tales, myths, rites, and art work.

JUNGIAN SYMBOLS FOR INTERPRETING THE PSYCHE

Jung felt that a person experiences the unconscious through various symbols encountered in all aspects of their life, such as in dreams, religion, art, and the symbolic dramas enacted in both relationships and life pursuits and activities. Examples include the following:

- Personal -- The mask humans present to the world around them
- Shadow -- The conscious self's repressed and suppressed aspects, which may be a shadow's constructive and destructive types.
- Anima and animus -- Archetypes that are feminine and masculine and guide one to their unconscious unified self.
- Self-Regulating center of a person that unifies opposites. It fully develops in what Jung termed "individuation".
- Hero -- The individual found in common myths in all cultures who performs various extraordinary tasks, such as slaying dragons or rescuing children from burning buildings.

JUNG'S VIEWS ON THE MANDALA

The mandala (a Sanskrit word for magic circle), in Jungian psychology, symbolizes breaking down the originals chaotic unity into four basic elements (water, earth, wind, fire), and then combining them into higher unity. Carl G. Jung's Mandala Symbolism explores the therapeutic value of significance of creating a mandala. Jung viewed the mandala as a symbol of completeness, wholeness, and perfection, and that it symbolized the self. Jung's interest in mandalas began while he was studying Eastern religions. He viewed the circular images his patients experienced as "movement towards psychological growth, expressing the idea of a safe refuge, inner reconciliation and wholeness." Jung considered mandalas to be "vessels" into which humans project their psyche, which is then returned as a means of restoration. Jung recognized that archetypes used in many cultures appeared in a mandala's spontaneous expression of the client's unconscious.

FAMILY SYSTEMS THERAPY

Family Systems Therapy is a psychotherapy method that examines the complex system or a family as a whole, with its own language, beliefs, roles, rules, patterns, and needs. Each member of the family plays a role in the system. Family System Therapy focuses on assisting an individual to discover how the family functions, the individual's role in the system, and how the role affects that individual in his or her relationships within the family and with others.

The following are some unifying concepts underlying the various family systems therapies:

- Humans are a product of their environment and social context.
- Personality development results from current familial interactions rather than the individual psyche.

- The best clinical treatment method is to alter the individual's family interactions.
- The "patient" is the entire family.

NATHAN ACKERMAN

Ackerman is considered a pioneer in the family therapy field and is credited with forming the concept of family psychology. Ackerman believed that one family member's mental or physical disposition impacts other family members. He advocated strongly for treating the whole family to solve the individual's problems. Ackerman described a healthy family using the term "homodynamic principle". Every family has their own basic dynamic.

Healthy families have stability and structure to allow them to change and adapt as new situations arise and the family ages. A dysfunctional family is not able to adapt and may have problems such as poor behavior, learning disabilities, and parental abuse, which are various defenses used by individual family members. Family therapy aims to promote communication that is freer and more open and improve problem-solving techniques.

JAY HALEY

Jay Haley developed strategic, humanistic therapy approaches. His therapy method emphasized creative and provocative instructions for patients to react to, with the goal of stopping problematic behavior sequences and replacing them with ones that are more functional and flexible. He pioneered several innovations for educating and training therapists, favoring teaching specific skills to enable individuals to deal directly with their problems, instead of engaging in drawn-out family background discussions as a means of identifying their problems. Haley was the first to video record therapy sessions as a means to review the techniques used by future therapists, and was the first to observed therapists-in-training using one-way mirrors.

SALVADOR MINUCHIN

Minuchin developed Structural Family Therapy (SFT), which focused on the family's structure and substructures. Minuchin felt that a family is either functional or dysfunctional depending on its ability to adapt to various developmental and extra-familial stressors. In healthy families, boundaries between parents and children are clear and semi-diffuse, while in dysfunctional ones, antisocial behavior patterns are considered necessary to maintain the structure of the family. Minuchin strived to restructure the family system to make it healthier by entering the different family subsystems and trying to revise the system. The revision introduced to the system was designed to advance the family from being stuck in nagging, self-pity, self-blame, and anorexia to a more creative and adaptable one.

MURRAY BOWEN

Dr. Bowen is credited as being the first to recognize and assert that a family as a unit is greater than the sum of its constituent parts. He described the family unit as a system of interconnected and interdependent people, whom cannot be understood in isolation apart from the system as a whole. Families function in predictable manners and generate energy and a culture that impacts every member in turn. A change in one member's functioning is predictably and reciprocally followed by changes in the others' functioning. When one family member carries or takes on too much responsibility for the issues or distress of other members in the family, then the family as a whole becomes more vulnerable to issues such as physical illness, depression, alcoholism, or affairs.

HANNA KWIATKOWSKA

Hanna Kwiatkowska, an art therapy pioneer, emerged in the 1950s and authored a work titled Family Therapy and Evaluation Through Art. Kwiatkowska worked the National Institute of Mental Health, where she used her knowledge as an artist and translated it to the field of family social work. There, she introduced art therapy evaluation and treatment techniques, and developed a structured procedure for evaluating families. The procedure consists of a one meeting with all available nuclear family members. The family is tasked to create a series of drawings (such as a family picture, an abstract family portrait, an open-ended picture, a joint family drawing, etc.), then discuss and evaluate the meaning of the work. Kwiatkowska's evaluation is considered one of the first standardized evaluation procedures that an art therapist developed.

GESTALT THERAPY
FRITZ PERLS

Gestalt therapy was developed and popularized by Fritz Perls, with the goal of raising clients' awareness of how they function in their various environments (work, school, home, etc.) with family or friends. Gestalt therapy focuses mainly on what is happening in the moment, rather than the content being discussed. One of Perls' goals was to help people own their experiences and develop into a healthy whole person, termed a Gestalt. Perls put emphasized the individual's responsibility in therapy and employed the "here-and-now" idea to unify feelings, thoughts, and actions.

GESTALT THERAPY TECHNIQUES

Some of the Gestalt techniques employed in therapy include:

- *Staying with the Feeling* – A technique that encourages the client to maintain their current reported feeling to build their capacity to deepen a feeling and work through it to completion.
- *Enactment (empty chair, hot seat)* -- A technique where an individual puts thoughts or feelings into action to increase awareness, rather than for cathartic purposes.
- *Exaggeration* -- A technique that asks a person to exaggerate some thought, feeling, movement, etc., to increase its perceived intensity or vision.

31

- *Guided Fantasy* – A technique where the client more efficiently brings an experience into the present by first visualizing, then enacting. Recreation of the fantasy as an actual lived event attempts to help the client get in better touch with the fantasy.
- *"It/You Talk"* – A technique where clients say "you" or "it" in place of "I."

JANIE RHYNE

As explained in Rhyne's *The Gestalt Art Experience,* he aimed to apply Gestalt therapy techniques to art work. Rhyne believed humans have an inherent desire to create things. Gestalt art experience-created forms become an extension or manifestation of that desire. The client in Gestalt art experience is left to decide the how, why, and what of making the art form. The art that unfolds is as unique as the individual who makes it.

Gestalt art experience client goals include:

- Create art forms
- Get involved in the art forms being made as events
- Observe the creation process
- Via graphic productions, perceive an individual's present self and different available ways to create one's goal self.

INFLUENCE OF GESTALT PSYCHOLOGY ON CONTEMPORARY PSYCHOLOGY

One of the main beliefs of Gestalt theorists is that the whole is always greater than the sum of the constituent parts. The theory's focus is the notion of "grouping" the ways in which people tend to interpret a visual field or problem.

Factors used to determine grouping include:

- Proximity - Items are often grouped together based on their nearness to one another.
- Similarity –Items that have similar characteristics or are related are often grouped together.
- Closure - Items that complete some entity are often are grouped together.
- Simplicity - Items that can be organized into simple figures based on regularity, symmetry, and smoothness are often grouped together.

The therapist helps guide the client through the process of the art experience by raising probing questions that will allow the client to acknowledge and integrate the various parts of the art form. The process' goal is for the client to use his or her artwork as a way to perceive current self and discover different available ways to create his or her goal self.

CARL ROGERS

Carl R. Rogers is considered the father of therapy that is client-centered or non-directive. His work impacted many areas, ranging from leadership and education to parent-child relationships and marriage. Rogers referred to client-centered therapy as counseling and stressed that its goal was for the patient to direct each session's focus and pace. He believed that all humans possess an innate desire to learn, grow, and develop their talents and abilities to the fullest. Rogers felt the therapist's role was to form somewhat of a personal relationship with the client and the patient reach a state of realization such that they can better help themselves. Rogers thought that growth occurs when an individual addresses and works to overcome their problems, and develops new insights and coping skills. Client-Centered Therapy is focused on expanding self-awareness, self-esteem, and self-reliance.

Rogers identified the following three qualities that every client-centered therapist should possess:

- *Empathy* -- The therapist should be able to feel the emotions the client is experiencing but remain free from entanglement of the feelings. Reflection and clarification are the two processes that foster empathic understanding. When reflecting, the therapist repeats parts of the client's report or words nearly verbatim to demonstrate listening and understanding. In clarification, the therapist uses the client's statements to extrapolate the gist.
- *Congruence* -- The therapist should always strive for honesty and genuineness with the patient.
- *Unconditional positive regard* -- The therapist should respect and accept how the client feels as a way to create a psychologically safe atmosphere in the counseling session. Low self-esteem frequently ensues when authority figures in the patient's life have made to feel that they are lacking in some way.

B. F. Skinner

In the 1950s and 1960s, B.F. Skinner popularized the learning theory of operant conditioning, which is founded on the idea that learning results from behavioral changes. These behavioral changes are caused by an individual's response to stimuli (events) occurring in their environment.

Positive or negative reinforcement is used to encourage a person to behave in a desired manner, so that the person learns to associate the reinforcement's pleasure or pain with the target behavior. Skinner's operant conditioning learning theory forms most behavior therapies' foundations and has been successfully used by art therapists working with children with disabilities, phobias, and anxieties. Various reward and punishment techniques, such as guided imagery, aversion therapy, and desensitization may be employed by the therapist.

The following are some of the basic tenants of operant conditioning:

- *Stimulus-response* a learning method that results from associating an external stimulus (an experience) and a behavioral response (the subsequent reaction). This learning approach omits any cognitive or mental processing.

- *Behavioral conditioning* is a type of psychological principle that asserts that a behavior's frequency can be increased or decreased using reward, punishment, and other stimuli association.
- *Behavior modification* is a therapy form used to change behavior based on Skinner' operant conditioning principles. It is necessary to carefully observe those events preceding and following the target behavior. Manipulations to the environment help reinforce the desired responses and behavior change. This form of therapy has been used on a variety of psychological problems and appears to work well with pediatric patients.

CRISIS INTERVENTION

Crisis intervention methods provide immediate, short-term assistance to individuals who have experienced an event that lead to emotional, mental, behavioral, or physical distress or issues. Brief psychotherapy addressing the "here-and-now" with the goal to helping the individual regain pre-crisis stability forms the basic treatment. Crisis intervention is intended for those clients in immediate danger of decompensation to decrease anxiety, identify present stressors, and employ internal and external factors to reduce stress levels. Such treatment usually lasts approximately six weeks, a time frame that is selected based on the idea that when individuals are in the midst of a crisis, they are most open to change. The therapist's role is to be supportive and active. Some examples of common crisis intervention modalities include telephone hotlines, community-based mental health, and hospital-based crisis intervention.

BASIC TECHNIQUES UTILIZED IN CRISIS INTERVENTION

The emergency situation addressed by crisis intervention is divided into the following four steps:

- *Assessment*: To best guide the planning process for the intervention and treatment, the caregiver pinpoints the primary problem the patient is experiencing, its severity, events that precipitated its occurrence, the patient's coping ability, the length of time the problem has persisted, and its impact on other people.
- *Determination of the therapeutic intervention*: The patient's caregiver determines the services necessary for treatment, such as outpatient referrals, psychiatric treatment (voluntary or involuntary), and treatment recommendation provisions for chemically-dependent patients.
- *Intervention*: The treatment for the individual.
- *Resolution*: The patient is restored to their previous (or improved) level of psychological equilibrium on the mental health scale.

SUICIDAL/HOMICIDAL IDEATION

It is important to take all suicidal and homicidal ideation and/or planning seriously. This type of behavior is considered a psychiatric emergency necessitating immediate evaluation and treatment. Intervention entails alleviating the patient's immediate discomfort and desperation as a way to "buy time" and consider alternative treatments. The caregiver or caregiving team performs a medical and an extended suicide evaluation, the outcome of which helps determine the appropriate referral for continued crisis work, hospitalization, or discharge plan for the patient. The main reason for hospitalization is to protect the patient and others and permit trained staff to help the patient explore what factors initiated the suicidal crisis and to identify alternative solutions.

The following signs must be taken seriously:

- Final plan formations
- Direct verbal warnings
- Acutely depressed behavior
- Social behavior changes
- History of suicidal behavior or ideation
- Drug and alcohol use
- The patient's close friend or family member's intuition and concern

ANXIETY ATTACKS

Anxiety attacks may either arise gradually overtime or quite suddenly, and they may persist for any length of time. The severity of anxiety ranges from mild to severe and even panic. It can be difficult to diagnose anxiety because of the wide variety of causes as well as the highly individualized nature of its symptom manifestation. An individual's severity may move around the continuum. Human anxiety examples include obsessions, phobic disorders, compulsions, and many other forms. Most care has the goal of helping the patient reduce his or her anxiety to manageable levels. Most patients presenting with anxiety are prescribed some type of psychotherapy with medication.

ADVERSE DRUG REACTIONS

Adverse drug reactions can initially result in concerning physical problems like intoxication, withdrawal, etc. Additionally, physical effects may include shock, respiratory depression, cardiovascular collapse, temperature fluctuations, seizures, and renal problems.

Before crisis intervention can begin, the patient and caregiver's safety and health considerations must be prioritized. The National Institute on Drug Abuse has demonstrated that crisis interventions that involve drugs and alcohol do not necessarily need the client's initial willingness in order to effectuate positive change over time. The counseling approach termed Living in Balance (LIB) is designed to be a practical, instructional guide about conducting group-oriented sessions for treating people with drug abuse or addiction issues.

People with active substance abuse problems are usually better served at specifically designed substance abuse facilities.

DOMESTIC VIOLENCE

Crisis interventions to help victims of domestic violence should do the following:

- Encourage and assist the victim in seeking medical attention.
- Provide the patient information to keep themselves safe in the future and information about domestic violence in general.
- Provide the patient with information about a person's legal rights
- Explore option with the patient.
  - Report the domestic violence to the proper authorities and press appropriate charges against the batterer.
  - Help the patient move out temporarily or permanently
  - Insist that the partner who is abusive move out temporarily or permanently.
  - Encourage the victim to seek professional counseling and care.

Many professionals believe that short-term counseling along with advocacy is necessary to treat victims of domestic violence successfully. However, in many cases, a long-term approach is necessary to work through the abuse and prevent future abusive relationships.

RAPE

Rape crisis programs offer the following help to victims:

- Accompaniment to navigate the police, medical, and legal systems.
- Ongoing supportive behavioral or CBT counseling to work through delayed effects of the sexual assault or abuse.
- Deliver programs on prevention and education to reduce adult and children sexual assault risk.
- Offer 24-hour crisis line staffed by volunteer trained advocates.

Services are confidential for all those except children under 18 years of age, the elderly, or fully-dependent adults. By law, it is required to report these victims to Adult Protective Services or to the Children Services Division.

PREVENTIVE INTERVENTIONS

The term "prevention" is generally applied broadly to interventions that occur before a disorder's initial onset. Areas addressed by preventative interventions include:

- Stress exposure --Target already affected or at-risk infants, children, adolescents, and/or their caregivers
- Resource access -- Provide interventions that target improving mental health and preventing behavior problems, such as The Primary Mental Health Project (PMHP), which is a program designed for early detection and prevention of school adjustment problems of young children. Medicaid, and Drug or HIV programs are other examples.

- Effective resource use -- Provide specific resources like community media, educational campaigns, or information to improve parenting skills and address negative behaviors like drug use, delinquency, dropping out of school, and violence.

The most popular crisis intervention models such as debriefing and crisis counseling are not typically offered until hours or days post-event. To offset emotional distress effects such as overexcitement, severe fear, misdirected anger, and anxiety, psychological first aid (PFA) is offered to help people right after the crisis. The Institute of Medicine of the National Academies defines PFA as, "...a set of skills identified to limit distress and negative health behaviors (e.g., smoking) that can increase fear, arousal and subsequent health care utilization."

BASIC CONCEPTS OF INTERVENTIONS:
- Address the patient's immediate medical and physical needs
- Comfort and console any affected individuals
- Provide specific information about where to get help
- Listens to and validates the individual's feelings
- Link individuals to available support systems
- Normalize or validate stress reactions to sudden loss and trauma
- Reinforce positive coping mechanisms

BRIEF THERAPY
Brief therapy is frequently called crisis intervention. It is used to help people deal with specific crises in their lives (death, illness diagnosis, etc.). Brief therapy can also be implemented episodically over years for long-term problems like trauma or severe abuse. Many therapists and researchers consider 30 therapy sessions to be "brief", though other therapists refer to significantly fewer sessions.

Brief therapy must:

- Have goals that are time-limited
- Define issues as temporary and modifiable
- Be manageable within the allotted time
- Include interventions that are goal-directed
- Be prioritized by the therapist
- Be focused or targeted to a specific area of the patient's life
- Be positively stated so the patient can control his or her desired changes
- Have tasks that are structured
- Assign directives and homework that one can do independently

BRIEF THERAPY AND EXTERNAL DISASTER/EMERGENCY
Reactions to disasters may range from acute disturbances like heavy sweating, trembling, overactivity (fast talk, joking, panic, vomiting) depression, nausea, and/or numbness. It is relativity common for an injured person to be unaware or minimize their injury in the immediate aftermath of a disaster, accident, or act of

violence. It is important to remember that medical emergencies must always be prioritized over psychological or behavioral ones.

Optimally, crisis intervention services are provided within 12 to 72 hours after the event to the patient. Two key goals of immediate response to external traumas and/or emergencies or disasters are:

- Normalizing feelings -- provide reassurance to victims that their post-event strange and upsetting are normal
- Assisting victims in finding effective coping mechanisms for their ongoing stresses.

IMAGERY AND CRISIS

Emotional reactions to different crises vary in their nature and severity, often dependent on age, previous experiences, personality and temperament, and the immediacy or acuteness of the crisis to the person's own life. When patients' lives are disrupted by a crisis, commonly displayed behaviors include self-centered concerns for safety, food, and clothing, stages of grief, and loss of control and stability. Resulting mental imagery can include "seeing in one's mind's eye," "hearing in one's head," and/or one "imagining the feel (etc.) of"). Patients often understand imagery experiences as echoes, reconstructions, or copies of actual past perceptual experiences. They may also seem to anticipate possible, frequently feared or desired, future experiences. Art therapy affords the patient the opportunity to record and explore the thoughts and contents of the images.

Art can make visible difficult or painful things to see or verbalize, such as traumatic memories and unresolved developmental or relationship issues. The process of art therapy can trigger mental imagery, which, in the absence of the appropriate or helpful external stimuli, can cause discomfort and emotional retreat. If this overwhelms an individual's available coping mechanisms, disequilibrium and then a crisis results. Crisis theory operates on the basic assumption that a crisis can cause one can to either advance or regress, depending upon how it is managed. Thus, the therapist needs to recognize the pre-crisis state signs and symptoms and be knowledgeable about techniques for management to assist personal coping, and design appropriate interventions for their patients.

ASSESSING CRISIS IMPACT

Usually, the crisis impact assessment takes the form of an informal interview, during which the therapist strives to foster an atmosphere of acceptance, support, and reassurance about the future. It is vital to have positive communication with the individual experiencing the crisis and use eye contact. Questions for the individual may include their perception of the problem, their feelings, the frequency and timeline of events, and a treatment history. To assess communication ability, close- or open-ended questions may be used; it is not uncommon for one to experience difficulty in self-expression, making decisions, or solving problems.

IMPACT OF HMOs

Psychotherapy practice has been affected in many important ways by health maintenance organizations (HMOs), which are managed care firms. These organizations lower the costs associated with mental health care in the following ways:

- They limit the paid annual number of therapy sessions for each insured individual.
- They determine the number of allotted therapy sessions for each patient by assigning a case reviewer.
- They pay a set fee to therapists to meet with a patient for up to a determined maximum number of sessions based on the problem, without interference from case reviewers. For the therapist, this creates a financial incentive to reduce the length of treatment.
- The patient must select their therapist from a list approved by their HMO.
- The patient is not assured complete confidentiality because case reviewers receive treatment plans and progress notes.
- They favor psychopharmacology over therapy.

INDIVIDUAL THERAPY

Most people seek individual therapy for their problems over group or other forms of therapy. Individual therapy enables the therapist to focus exclusively on the patient's personal problems with more privacy and confidentiality than afforded in a group setting. Individual therapy involves sessions between a patient and his or her therapist. Particulars of individual therapy sessions such as the duration, seating arrangement, frequency, etc., vary across different types of therapy.

Individual therapy is often recommended for first-time patients as a way to more gently and personally-tailor the introduction to the therapy experience. The patient may subsequently move on to other forms of therapy or even add an additional form of therapy to his or her initial therapy treatment plan.

STAGES OF TREATMENT

The following are stages of treatment:

- Stage 1 -- Stabilize the patient
- Behavioral control is achieved by decreasing life-threatening behaviors and those behaviors that interfere with therapy sessions, such as missing sessions, lateness, poor follow through, etc.
- Quality-of-life interfering behaviors should be reduced by decreasing behavioral patterns substantial enough to markedly interfere with any likely chance of a decent quality of life, such as depression, homelessness, or substance dependence.
- Positive behavioral skills should be increased, such as those skills in emotion regulation, distress tolerance, interpersonal effectiveness, self-management, and mindfulness.

- Stage 2 -- Help the client replace "quiet desperation" with an emotional experience that is non-traumatic
- Stage 3 -- Resolve living problems and any residual disorders to attain "ordinary" happiness
- Stage 4 -- Resolve any lingering sense of incompleteness and help the patient achieve joy

ROLE OF GOAL SETTING

Individuals are able to be rational and take responsibility for their actions but they may need guidance and motivation to do so. The therapist may act as the "confronter," prompting the patient to examine the problem and require them to make a commitment to forming a plan to address the problem in a clearly-defined course. This plan not only the problematic behavior(s), but it also insists on a commitment from the patient (and often the therapist) for problem remediation. A contract clearly describes the role of the patient and his or her therapist in the most effective problem-solving process. The patient is ultimately responsible for the plan's success, but if the plan happens to fail, the therapist then assumes control until a new plan is developed. Typically, behavioral contracts do not state consequences for failure. They may be designed with both the patient as well as others involved in his or her life.

DESIGNING A PLAN FOR PATIENT NEEDS IN INDIVIDUAL THERAPY

The assessment information and the general framework for evidence-based best practices are used to develop the patient's individualized treatment plan. This plan undergoes continual revisions, based on changes or events that occur during the course of treatment. Program participants and those close to them are encouraged to participate in the development and evolution of a plan. The therapist, with as much patient involvement as possible, determines the diagnosis, treatment form, initial goals, and treatment strategies.

The intake process should yield a plan approved by both the patient and therapist as to approximate duration of therapy, frequency, auxiliary support needs, primary treatment focus, or possible referral.

All treatment plans should include the following:

- Short-term goals
- Long-term goals
- Goal achievement plan
- Goal measurement methods
- Periodic evaluation plan

THE EVALUATION PROCESS

Insurance reimbursement requires the patient have a psychological diagnosis. All psychological treatment submitted for insurance reimbursement starts with a diagnostic evaluation to identify the appropriate clinical diagnosis for the patient. This assessment involves questions about the problem itself, personal and family history of the patient, and a survey of current life stressors. Psychological providers use a host of verbal assessments to determine whether there a specific psychological problem appears to exist. Once such problems are identified, an effective treatment plan can be developed. The diagnostic process is ongoing during psychotherapy, as the practitioner reassess symptoms, problems, and progress, and reviews other possible treatments.

REVIEW PROCEDURES

As managed care gains popularity, more patients may find their psychotherapy coverage abruptly cut off, potentially placing the therapist in a litigious situation. The professional code of ethics provides the information about terminating therapy including the following:

- Psychologists can terminate therapy treatment when it becomes reasonably evident that the patient:
  - no longer needs the therapy
  - is unlikely to benefit from the therapy
  - is being harmed by continued therapy
- Other reasons for termination include:
  - Threats or feelings of endangerment toward the therapist from the patient or another individual associated with the patient, except in cases where precluded by the patient or third-party payor's actions prior to termination, therapists should provide pre-termination counseling and referrals or suggestions of alternative service providers, if necessary.

ISSUES THAT CONTROL THE THERAPEUTIC RELATIONSHIP

- *Transference* -- The unconscious assignment of feelings and attitudes toward others that were originally associated with other important figures in an individual's life. The psycho-dynamically-oriented provider uses this to help the patient understand the origins or underpinnings of their emotional problems.
- *Countertransference* -- A psychotherapist's conscious or unconscious emotional responses to a patient; it is the therapist's responsibility to monitor their reactions and minimize their impact on the patient's treatment and the therapeutic relationship.
- *Boundaries* -- For the safety and comfort of the patient, therapist, and other involved outsiders, it is important to establish professional behavioral boundaries, such as a fee schedule, session length, session appointment time, personal disclosure, physical contact limits, and the professional relationship's general tone.

AUTONOMY AND DEPENDENCE IN INDIVIDUAL THERAPY

Autonomy refers to one's freedom to choose and assume responsibility for one's personal acts. This principle states that an individual's independent actions and choices should not be made or constrained by others. Dependence, the opposite, is the need for emotional support, comfort, attention, nurturance, care, and similar responses received from significant others. For young children, dependent behaviors may involve clinging to parents, crying or whining when caregivers depart, and seeking physical proximity to caregivers. Older children, adolescents, and adults may more symbolically express their need for positive support from loved ones in times of distress by seeking approval, reassurance, comfort, affection, or solace. Dependence can be viewed as a continuum with autonomy and dependence on opposite ends.

ROLE OF FAMILY-OF-ORIGIN

The family into which an individual is born and is raised form interactions with the individual that can either perpetuate and exacerbate a problem or assist in resolving it. For example, some families scapegoat one of their members, which can undermine that member's treatment in individual therapy. Individual symptoms are frequently seen as family problems and as such, the family and the individual both need to be treated. Accordingly, many therapists conduct individual therapy sessions for one or more family members at the same time that they and the whole family together for therapeutic sessions.

METAPHORS IN CLIENT'S ART

Art becomes a vehicle for emotional expression as it offers metaphors for the individual's issues. These metaphors connect individuals both to their own self and to others, affording insight, guidance, and healing. Metaphors' use in art therapy can offer a means for patients to explore difficult problems, which they may have not previously verbalized to themselves or others. Evaluating the metaphor that emerges in one's art, allows the individual to directly respond to his or her imagery. It allows the therapist to more personally shape an intervention for the patient's situation.

COUPLES THERAPY

The term "couples" has mostly replaced "marital" in an effort to include the increasing number of people who cohabitate in a committed relationship but are either not yet married or have chosen not to marry. The focus of couples' therapy is on the existing problems in two people's relationship. These relational problems involve individual symptoms and problems and relationship conflicts. The therapist's role is to identify the areas of conflict within the relationship and help guide the couple to determine needed behavioral changes. Couples therapy is frequently paired with family therapy due to the similar topics addressed in both forms.

RESOLVING CONFLICTS IN MARITAL/COUPLES THERAPY

Couples therapy often involves improving effective communication and listening skills. Couples must identify common life goals, skills in avoiding competing with each other and how to share responsibilities. Regardless of which partner is suffering more, the therapist should be sensitive to the needs and feelings of all involved clients. The therapist continually looks for flawed communication patterns that may disrupt the relationship. Different techniques may be implemented to directly focus on communication skill-building. Listening techniques may include reflection of feelings, restatement of content, taking turns to expressing thoughts and feelings, and nonjudgmental brainstorming. In some cases, the therapist may try to teach a couple how to listen and communicate fairly, or how to express themselves.

Couples seeking counseling often explicitly ask for help in resolving the conflicts and issues that have created relational tensions. Conflict resolution is the process of forming an action plan that addresses and resolves issues in dispute. It starts by clarifying the initial positions or differences of each party and their preferred course of action. Then, both sides work together to explore and evaluate the underlying concerns that have resulted in their respective positions. Finally, couples work to create a solution that considers both participants' concerns.

MEDIATION IN COUPLES THERAPY

Mediation is a collaborative and voluntary process where individuals in conflict with one another identify problems, generate options, consider alternatives, and create a consensual agreement. Open communication is facilitated by trained mediators to help resolve differences in a confidential and non-adversarial manner. The mediator facilitates discussion, which should focus on the future and help the involved parties reach fair and enforceable agreements. The primary mediation goals include:

- Reduce communication obstacles between participants
- Address all involved participants' needs
- Maximize the identification of alternatives
- Help guide participants to find their own resolution
- Offer a proven conflict resolution model for future issues

The mediator should not be tasked with finding a solution and making the disputing individuals abide by it. Instead, the goal of mediation is to help the disputing individuals work together to determine a solution themselves that they can live with.

DIVORCE MEDIATION IN COUPLES THERAPY

The process of separation and divorce invites anger, fear, revenge, depression, and anxiety that are often best dealt with by the therapist. The process of divorce mediation involves discussing and forming a written agreement on divorce issues regarding children, finances, and property. The discussions are facilitated with a professional mediator. Both members of the splitting couple participate in the process.

The divorce mediation process typically characterized by the following:

- Voluntary: The process is always non-coercive.
- Full Disclosure: The involved parties must consent to full disclosure.
- Fairness: It is expected that the agreement will be "fair" to both parties.

- Confidential: The sessions take place in a confidential setting.
- Mediator Impartiality: The mediator remains unbiased.

ROLE DEFINITION, GENDER, AND SEXUALITY IN COUPLES' THERAPY

Couples carry conflict to therapy sessions, often involving gender, role definition, and sexuality. Certain family roles may have become so ingrained or habitual that the surrounding or involved conflicts may be obscured. Differences in gender can affect communication style, the types of issues brought to counseling sessions, and the effective problem-solving approach. Additionally, many couples experience certain long-standing or persistent conflicts, like sexual issues, which can be tied to chronic tensions about male and female roles. Owing to cultural and family influences, individuals often experience guilt, embarrassment, and shame regarding sexuality. Sex therapy is often part of couple's therapy, because sexual issues between partners are frequently a problem. When other relational conflicts arise, a couple's sex life is often affected.

SETTING EFFECTIVE MUTUAL AND INDIVIDUAL GOALS IN COUPLES THERAPY

Relational problems usually include individual symptoms and issues and the relationship conflicts themselves. In the couple's therapy process, it is necessary to set both individual and mutual goals in order to improve the relationship in meaningful ways. The following are suggestions for helping clients set effective goals in couple's therapy:

- Ensure goals are as concrete and specific as possible.
- Ensure progress is measurable.
- Establish challenging, but realistic goals that will produce a sense of accomplishment.
- State goals in positive language. Partners often set negative goals, like "I don't want to feel sad."
- Set a range of timeframes, such as daily, weekly, yearly, etc. to achieve goals.
- Set goals across a variety of life areas, such as job, financial, therapy, or personal growth.
  - o Avoid establishing too many goals at one time because they may be forgotten or abandoned.

SAME - SEX COUPLES

Typically, the problems facing same-gender couples are the same or similar to those of heterosexual couples. However, most same-sex couples are not equally protected by marriage laws.

Issues commonly faced by same-sex couples include:

- Self-disclosure or "coming out" within their family of origin -- This is often the issue important to others in the individual's life. Fear or rejection and discrimination are concerns typically associated with sharing such information openly.

- Legal Issues -- Custody, recognition of dependents, and conflicts involving children in same-sex relationships present particular challenges because of the constant evolution of the legal ground for custody rights of same-sex couples. Issues frequently involve children from dissolved or broken heterosexual marriages or same-sex relationships.
- Parenting -- There may be issues of embarrassment by adolescents of their homosexual parents

THERAPEUTIC RELATIONSHIP HAZARDS

Freud employed the concepts of "transference" and "counter-transference" to address the strong emotions often projected by the patient onto the provider and vice versa, respectively.

- Transference -- While treating an analyst or provider like one's father may promote therapeutic work, Freud was also aware that it may distort the perspective of the patient and therapist.
- Idealization of the Therapist -- The patient excessively admiring the therapist may make patients vulnerable to the therapist exploiting them
- Dependency -- A patient's long-term involvement with an authoritarian therapist can increase their dependency and decrease their ability to make personal decisions or form new friendships unless the therapist explicitly grants approval
- Boundaries -- If a therapist involves a patient in his or her personal life, the patient may become their friend, student, employee, lover, etc.

FAMILY THERAPY

The following major concepts surround family systems theory:

- The "identified patient" is the symptomatic family member that has caused the family to seek treatment. Illness existing in one family member may be indicative of a family problem at large.
- Any major change in one family member affects the family structure as a whole and each member individually. The family as a unit usually attempts to maintain its organization and function, and resist change.
- Considering the extended family can often help explain the intergenerational transmission of different attitudes, problems, and behaviors.
- Familial emotional relationships typically involve three people. Triangular relationships, as they are called, often occur when two conflicting family members "triangle in" a third family member to try to stabilize their own relationship.

FAMILY THERAPY TECHNIQUES

Examples of family therapy techniques include:

- A genogram/family map delineates all relatives and pertinent information. It may reveal patterns and facts that can illuminate present issues.
- Sculpting is the patient's visual representation of their experience of their present family situation. The therapist is particularly interested in the placement and arrangement of others.
- The method of Reframing or reauthoring is used to alter the focus, and especially to draw attention away from the identified patient.
- Joining is a process used by the therapist to ally with family members by actively expressing interest in better understanding them as individuals and striving to work with and for their interests.
- Unbalancing is the process by which the therapist tries to support an individual or subsystem of participants against the family unit at large.
- Enactments/role playing involves families demonstrating problematic family situations by enacting them in therapy to the therapist for evaluation and guidance.
- Directives as homework may be tasked by family therapists to try and reveal significant patterns or bring about desired changes.

CONCEPTS OF DIFFERENTIATION

Family models consider individual problems in relation to other family members and attempt to remedy dysfunctional family patterns. Terms frequently used to describe familial relation include the following:

Differentiation -- the ability of each member of the family to maintain his or her own personal sense of self, while remaining connected emotionally to the family unit.

VIRGINIA SATIR

According to Virginia Satir, when one family member exhibits some symptom, it will affect all family members by becoming a sort of symptom sharing. Satir's work began emphasizing connections within families and expanded on group concepts--how individuals communicate and behave in groups. Satir also described several roles in families that often serve to stabilize expected familial behavior patterns. For example, if one child in the family is a "rebel", a sibling may assume the role of the "good" one to alleviate some familial stress. This role reciprocity concept is helpful in understanding family dynamics, as the complementary nature of roles often makes behaviors more resistant to necessary changes. Satir's humanistic and experiential and approach is termed the human validation process model.

HANNA KWIATKOWSKA

Kwiatowska, who designed the Family Art Evaluation instrument, is known for her family therapy use of graphic and plastic media. The evaluation involves a single meeting of all available nuclear family members. The family is tasked to create the following drawings or sketches:

1. a free drawing
2. a family drawing
3. an abstract family picture
4. a picture initiated by a scribble
5. a joint family scribble made together
6. a free scribble individually

After the drawings are completed, the art therapist facilitates a family discussion about the artwork product and the process of creating it. Kwiatkowska's evaluation is one of the first standardized evaluation procedures created by an art therapist.

SHIRLEY RILEY, BARBARA SOBOL, AND HELEN LANDGARTEN

Shirley Riley shaped art therapy programs' educational standards to include multicultural and diversity elements and developed educational standards for art therapy programs. Barbara Sobol is the Washington Art Therapy Studio director, which is a studio-model art therapy private practice focusing on child and adult survivors of domestic abuse in Washington D.C. Her clinical focus centers on trauma resolution and the development of the patient's artistic "voice."

Helen Landgarten, a Californian art therapist, developed the efficacy of using photographic collages as an assessment technique when working with patients and based on this medium, he created an assessment battery.

FAMILY DYNAMICS

Family dynamics, an Adlerian term, refers to the constant changes occurring in the familial interpersonal relationships or the ways that family members interact with each other and within the whole family. Family dynamics is a time-tested method of keeping the family united or linked via faith in one another, helping each other, raising confidence in members, mutual understanding and love, etc.

Individuals and subsystems exist within the family system. Examples of subsystems include siblings, spouses, or grandparents. The subsystems form alliances or coalitions and may share information, experiences, hopes, dreams, insider jokes, beliefs, or emotions.

FAMILY ROLES IN CONFLICT

Each family member plays a different role that has different expectations and responsibilities. Occasionally, one member of the family may view their roles and responsibilities in one certain way, while other family members view them very differently. These differing perceptions and expectations can cause confusion and frustration. Children can often assume familial roles to compensate for the parenting deficiencies. Families usually have one or more member in each of the following roles:

- Victim -- This individual's typical response to an issue is "I'm useless, and I'm unable to help myself. I need help."
- Persecutor -- This individual usually responds to the victim and other members by saying, "You are helpless and that is your fault."
- Rescuer -- This person's usual response to the victim is along the lines of "You are helpless and unable to help yourself. I'll try to help you out."

CONCEPTS REGARDING THE FAMILY

- Sibling rivalry -- Refers to hostility or antagonism between sisters and/or brothers that plays out in the common verbal or physical fights. Due to the natural competition that exists between siblings in most families, this conflict frequently develops into fights over both big and small things. In many instances, this competition is over their parents' time, attention, approval, and love.
- Generational conflict -- These types of conflicts concern differing expectations between households shared by parents and grandparents or with children reared by their grandparents.
- Identified patient -- The identified patient (IP) is the symptomatic family member that has caused the family to seek treatment. The IP is used by family therapists to prevent the family from scapegoating or using the IP as a means of avoiding other problems in the system.

DYSFUNCTIONAL FAMILY SYSTEMS

In a dysfunctional family, the relationships between the children and parents are strained and unnatural, often because one of the members has a serious problem. This problem impacts every other family member, who each feels constrained or pressured to adopt atypical roles that may allow the whole family to survive. A family system is considered functional when it can maintain itself and satisfy the individual needs of all members.

A dysfunctional family may successfully function as a system, but it fails to satisfy the developmental needs of its individual members. It also responds to internal or external change demands by stereotyping its functionality. The perception of children regarding their place in the family frequently influences how the children feel about themselves as well as how they interact with other people, which can affect their coping and relating styles.

FAMILY DRAWINGS

In family therapy, art therapy can provide an effective vehicle for perception sharing within the family, aided by the generational leveling aspect inherent to art expression. Most children feel comfortable making art and find it to be a useful way to make their thoughts heard within the family unit—a feeling that may not occur in their normal verbal family interactions. Differences among family members in their art expressiveness can positively change the family hierarchical structure. Submissive, withdrawn, or intimidated family members may benefit from art therapy serving as a new expression medium. Art therapy may open space within a family unit for role and position movement of its members. Family drawings or sketches provide an accessible, concrete, and external graphic representation of treatment progress. Art directives frequently include a family genogram, drawing boundaries, and a verbal and nonverbal family art task.

REVIEW OF MAJOR THERAPY TYPES

The following are some of the main types of therapy:

- *Group therapy* – psychosocial treatment form of regularly-scheduled meetings with a small group of patients who discuss problems with one another and the therapist, who serves as the group leader.
- *Cognitive-behavioral* – a type of therapy that focuses on changing one's beliefs, thoughts, and images in order to modify maladjusted behaviors. This type of therapy is goal-directed, occurs in brief meetings, focuses on symptom elimination and modification of specific maladjusted cognitions.
- *Gestalt* - a humanistic type of therapy that focuses on gaining an awareness of one's present emotions and behaviors rather than those in the past.
- *Psychodynamic* - a type of therapy that assumes unconscious, internal conflicts are at the root of improper or undesirable behavior. Therapy focuses on gaining insight and reflecting on these motivations.

It is important to note that *gestalt and psychodynamic therapies* use the psychoanalytic concepts of transference, parataxic distortion, mirroring, projection, and splitting.

GROUP THERAPY
DIRECTIVE AND NONDIRECTIVE TECHNIQUES

Techniques used in group therapy are varied and tend to focus on alleviating family members' distress by direct methods (called the directive approach) or creating a group atmosphere that is conducive to increasing each participants' self-understanding and personal growth.

In the directive approach, the goal is to increase members' morale and decrease feelings of isolation. This goal is accomplished by building a sense of group belongingness via testimonials, slogans, public recognition of members' progress, and rituals. Alcoholics Anonymous is an example.

The method that instead emphasizes the creation of a positive group atmosphere relies on nondirective or psychoanalytic techniques and aims to generate free discussion and uninhibited self-exploration. Most methods utilize face-to-face groups with five to eight members who are experiencing similar problems. Improved self-understanding and positive behavior of members is afforded through mutual examination and discussion of their reactions and interactions with people in their daily lives in an emotionally-supportive atmosphere with the group leader (therapist)

Special techniques are often especially useful in helping patients develop social skills, express their feelings, solve problems, resolve emotional conflicts, or reduce anxiety. Patients in the unstructured approach may choose from a variety of materials and media (such as clay, paint, or pastels) and use them in whatever way they choose, allowing unconscious thoughts and feelings surface. The therapist in the structured or directed approach may ask the patient to create or draw something specific like a family portrait, which can help expose complex family dynamics such as unhealthy relationships or poor communication methods.

IRVIN YALOM

Books authored by Irvin Yalom include his 1970 *The Theory and Practice of Group Psychotherapy* (later revised) and his 1980 *Existential Psychotherapy*. In Yalom's classic book, *Theory and Practice of Group Psychotherapy,* he identified eleven primary group therapy "therapeutic factors", each of which has particular importance for patients with substance abuse problems and each which can be used to help understand why a group operates in a particular way. The curative factors that Yalom defined to be associated with group psychotherapy specifically address issues such as the instillation of hope, group members' universal experiences, the opportunity to develop and improve insight through relationships, and other such concerns specific to supporting substance-abusing patients in their recovery. In psychotherapy, Yalom was an influential proponent of using the existential approach.

GROUP PROCESS STAGES

The development of a group is often viewed as having four distinct stages:

- *Forming* – When the group first comes together, members tend to be very polite, guarded in personal opinions, fairly reserved, with little conflict and leaders begin to emerge.
- Note: These characteristics may persist with members that are more nervous and/or subordinate
- *Storming* – In this stage, factions form, personalities may clash, and communication can be poor as no one is actively listening. Some members are still unwilling to openly talk.
- *Norming* – In this stage, sub-groups recognize and understand the merits of cooperation and working together. The conflicts and fighting subsides and members start to feel secure in sharing their views, listening improves, and the group as a whole establish and recognize work methods.
- *Performing* – This is the culmination stage where the group has settled on a system that allows free and open exchange of viewpoints and significant group support for each member and their decisions.

GROUP ROLE DEFINITION

All groups create roles for their members to occupy that usually reflect family system roles (for example, someone acts as the father, mother, spoiled child). Individuals relate to one another in the context of their roles; role expectations are at least partly based on relationships in which the people are involved. Some common functions include the nurturer, scapegoat, gatekeeper, disciplinarian, victim, and dominator, which are not necessarily assigned by gender. In some communities, for example, females have often carried out the "father" role, holding up standards and keeping things on track.

Therapist Acting as Group Leader -- Many people feel anxious or uneasy when considering joining a group and struggle to share personal feelings and thoughts with others. The therapist should aim to promote an atmosphere of safety, support, and trust so that group members feel secure in their self-disclosure. The therapist should be the non-judgmental witness and offer patient's whole acceptance. The therapist also fulfills the role of a facilitator, or the person who encourages and controls interactions within the group.

ROLE MODELING

Role modeling involves an individual visually demonstrating a desirable or undesirable behavior, thought, or attitude to the patient that he or she wants to change or acquire. Modeling is sometimes referred to as vicarious learning because the patient does not need to actually perform the behavior to learn it. Instead, he or she may simply be watching the behavior modeling. Role Modeling is quite effective when combined with reinforcement and role-play.

Types of modeling include the following:

- Live modeling -- Witnessing a real person (the therapist) enact a desired behavior that the patient has chosen to learn or modify.
- Symbolic modeling -- videotaped or filmed models, photographs, plays, and picture books.
- Participant modeling -- Anxiety-inducing behaviors modeled for the patient to engage in the behavior and work through it.
- Covert modeling -- patients are asked to use their imagination to visualize a particular behavior while the therapist describes the situation in detail.

SOCIAL SKILLS

Group therapy offers each member the opportunity to receive feedback from others who are experiencing similar problems. This feedback occurs in a trial social setting, which allows members a safe space to try newly-learned behaviors. As members engage in relationships, they acquire and practice new social skills that can help them reduce their isolation and connect meaningfully with others. Members also learn the important skill of how to disconnect, which can reduce grief- and loss-associated anxieties. At times, the group facilitator may deliberately focus on these social skills via role-playing or modeling activities within the group context. The intention is that the lessons acquired in therapy are practiced in clients' lives outside of the group setting.

VICTIM AND SCAPEGOAT

Most people do not like to blame themselves when problems occur. Therefore, they actively seek scapegoats to displace their aggression. The scapegoats may be individuals not "in" the group and are often people seen as powerless. Scapegoating usually increases when people feel frustrated and are seeking an available outlet for their anger. Once an individual is cast as a scapegoat, they cannot easily shake that classification. Scapegoating a person is to wrongfully and poorly treat them as though they caused issues that they did not cause and to treat them. A victim is an individual who is persecuted by another. The patient should not blame their past for their current situation and should not assume the victim role with no control over their present life.

GROUP SETTING SAFETY

A group is somewhat like being part of a family, such that participants tend to assume their familial roles. Rivalry, hostility, envy, support, anger, bonding, cohesiveness, helplessness, and concern all occur in the group therapy process. A skilled therapist should look out for these such problems and help maintain a feeling of safety for everyone in the group.

Providing a forum to actively explore group members' feelings in a safe setting allows the group members to consider how these feelings play out in their life outside the group. Participants who are suicidal, homicidal, sociopathic, psychotic, cognitively-impaired, or in the middle of a serious acute crisis are not usually referred for group therapy until both their behavior and emotional state have better stabilized.

AGGRESSION THEORIES

There are three basic aggression theories:

- The Biological-instinctual theory states that humankind is naturally aggressive, and "aggression" includes a range of behaviors. Many of these behaviors are constructive and essential to the individual's active existence.
- The Frustration theory states that aggression is a drive condition derived from interfering with ongoing purposeful activities. An individual feels frustrated when his or her expectations are violated, and then he or she tries to solve the problem via aggressive behavior. The frustration response is considered a learned behavior used to decrease the aggressive drive and eliminate the obstacle causing the frustration.
- Social-learning theory states that aggressive behavior is caused by child-rearing practices and other socialization forms instead of instinctual or frustration-produced inner drives. Aggressive behaviors may be acquired simply by watching and learning, often via imitation, and does not necessarily require frustration.

MASS PSYCHOLOGY

Mass psychology, or social psychology, studies the behaviors displayed in large groups of people. Adler argues that mass-psychology and the psychology of the individual must be considered from the same point of view. He believed that social groups of humans strive to overcome a minus-situation and maintain a strong tendency toward achieving social equality. Psychologists investigate how people's behaviors, thoughts, and feelings are influenced by the actual, implied, or imagined presence of other people. Specific research areas include aggression, persuasion and propaganda for the US military, racial prejudice, gender issues, and bystander intervention.

Psychoanalytic theory of the masses has the following basic assumptions:

- Dependency groups
- Fight or flight
- Pairing

USE OF MURALS

Mural creation is a helpful technique for groups of people experiencing similar issues. Group art therapy tasks are intended to enhance social bonding, sharing, problem-solving, and expressing emotions. The subject matter and material choices may be predetermined by the therapist or up to the group. In a larger group setting, this activity promotes group unity, cooperation, and self-expression. In some exercises, group members are tasked to make a mural together nonverbally, which allows members practice nonverbal communication skills and reduce barriers of isolation and distrust. After completion of the art project, the group members are given the opportunity to verbally express what they experienced during the creation process.

THERAPEUTIC APPROACHES

Therapeutic treatments include medical, inpatient, and educational approaches:

- The medical approach may work in cases where psychotherapies have failed to include medically-genetic factors. Drug therapies in those with mental disorders can reduce symptoms.
- Inpatient therapy focuses on stabilizing all crisis levels in an environment that is safe, secure, and structured. Treatment targets emergent symptoms and prepares clients for follow-up care in a setting that is less restrictive.
- Educational therapy is an effective method for children and adults that combines psychoanalytic and educational techniques. Stories, drawings, play, educational activities, and games are used to provide experiences that help the patients make sense of their difficulties and gain the necessary confidence to become an effective learner. Other educational programs are intended to address key issues of human behavior and development that are associated with addiction and subsequent recovery.

MEDICAL MODEL

Medical model includes set of doctor-developers and -trained procedures that includes complaint, history, examination, any needed ancillary tests, diagnosis, treatment, and the likely prognosis both with and without treatment. For treating emotional disorders, the medical model states that inappropriate behavior is symptomatic of an underlying cause. In conceptualizing the issue, the person exhibiting such behavior is understood to be disordered or "sick", such that the issue resides within the person. To treat such behavior, it may be necessary to identify and treat the underlying cause rather than the behavior itself, since the behavior is merely symptomatic.

PATIENT RIGHTS

Institutions and healthcare facilities establish policies and procedures to maintain patient information in strict confidentiality in compliance with the 1996 Health Insurance Portability and Accountability Act (HIPAA) stipulations. Topics commonly addressed for protected health information uses and disclosures include subjects such as the following:

- Protected health information use and disclosures with or without authorization
- Psychotherapy notes use and disclosure for research or other purposes
- Use and disclosure of protected health information for judicial or other administrative proceedings
- Protected health information uses and disclosures necessitating the opportunity to object or agree

Topics regarding patients' privacy rights for protected health information include items such as:

- Patient's right to amend their health information
- Notice regarding privacy practices
- The individual's access to their protected health information

BOUNDARIES IN THE THERAPEUTIC ENVIRONMENT

In therapy, there are two types of boundaries that are expressed in state and federal laws as well as professional codes of ethics. The first one is boundaries that surround the therapeutic relationship and the second is boundaries that are drawn between therapist and client. The first includes place of therapy, onset and termination of therapy, form of therapy, time and length of sessions, fees, confidentiality, incidental encounters outside the office and dual relationships. Boundaries of a second type are drawn between therapist and client and include issues such as physical touch, therapist's self-disclosure, gift exchange, (either from client to therapist, therapist to client or between therapist and a third party), language, silence, and physical proximity of therapist and client during sessions.

CODE OF ETHICS

Therapists need to maintain knowledgeable of and adhere to applicable professional laws and code of ethics. Some of these roles that are legally mandated roles include the following:

- Professional licensing listing grounds for license revocation or suspension (for example, false or misleading advertising, or relations with a patient).
- Protection reporting laws for the elderly, or dependent adults
- Psychotherapist/patient privileges that govern the actions of therapists regarding a patient's potential or real danger to themselves, others, or others' property.
- Defense against patient litigation
- Investigation conducted by a medical examiner to identify the patient's cause of death
- Health care oversight
- Patient-authorized disclosures
- Insurance fraud cases
- Patient's access to their medical records
- Rights of patients who are minors
- Alleged unethical conduct reporting

INSTITUTION LEGISLATION

A variety of distinct Federal entitlement programs shoulder much of a community's burden of supporting those with severe mental illness. The following are some of the major legislation affecting institutions:

- Medicaid and Medicare -- Medicaid permits states to shift elder care for those with behavioral symptoms from designated mental hospitals to long-term care nursing facilities
- Social Security Disability Insurance (SSDI) – Eligibility has expanded for disability benefits to cover individuals with some mental disabilities.
- Supplemental Security Income for the Aged, the Disabled, and the Blind (SSI) – Individuals whose disability or age renders them incapable of holding a job may receive income support.

These federal programs as well as food stamps and public housing programs allow individuals with severe and chronic mental illnesses to live in the community with the additional support from community mental health programs.

EXTERNALLY-SET GOALS

The shift in the mental health care pattern from an institutional-based to a community-based approach has significantly affected specialist mental health services as well as community services like primary health care providers, housing agencies, and community welfare agencies. Mental health service delivery is affected by reform movements and their ideologies, care and treatment advancements, and financial incentives determining the payer for different services. The complexity of mental health services has increased, as they are constantly being shaped by public policy and the advent of managed care, both which encourage short-stay hospitalization with subsequent community treatment.

PSYCHOTHERAPY AND ART THERAPY

Psychotherapy knowledge can be applied to the practice of art therapy in many ways including the following:

- Assessment and diagnostic usage
- Establishing a working relationship
- Verbalizing conscious or unconscious thoughts and feelings
- Helping deal with painful or disturbing symbolic material
- Developing interests that can be carried over into daily life, which will help strengthen future psychosocial development

Art therapy and verbal psychotherapy use the same underlying principles: Identifying a problem, getting the inside thoughts and feelings out, developing insight, discovering needed actions to change the involved dynamic, and applying learned material and tools. However, unlike therapy that is purely verbal, art therapy, from the start, is hands-on and action-oriented. Usually, an art therapy session consists of two parts: the art-making process and the art product exploration.

The term *psychotherapy* refers to the treatment of behavioral, emotional, psychiatric, and personality disorders based mainly on interventions and verbal or nonverbal communication with the patient, rather than chemical and physical treatments. Art therapy is a type of psychotherapy that employs art making as a central component of the therapeutic process. In art therapy, the patient uses paint, clay, and other art media to create works or images that explore their thoughts, feelings, fears, memories, or dreams. The art therapist's ability to assess and intervene with appropriate art tasks and materials is paramount to its therapeutic success.

ADJUNCTIVE VS. PRIMARY THERAPY

A patient's art therapist may function as either their primary or adjunctive therapist. When functioning as a primary therapist in a private practice, the art therapist helps clients communicate via nonverbal symbols and artistic expressions. When functioning as an adjunctive therapist, the art therapist operates as part of the multidisciplinary treatment team to relieve the patient's symptoms. Treatment is typically provided after the primary treatment with the intent of increasing the chances of relief.

ART THERAPY INTERVENTION STRATEGIES

Intervention strategies are specifically designed to encourage self-expression through creating art. The work produced is viewed as a tangible progress record made toward achieving treatment goals, and as an indication of the best direction for further therapeutic interventions. Art therapy intervention typically involves ongoing weekly group sessions. Intervention techniques may be spontaneous or more directed. Specific art therapy intervention techniques include the following examples: bridging exercises, anger resolution, feeling maps, self-image, basket weaving, loss and grief resolution, situational topics, journeys, collage, and reviewing previous art work.

IMPORTANCE OF DIAGNOSIS

Two commonly used diagnostic classifications systems include:

- The International Statistical Classification of Diseases and Related Health Problems (ICD) provides various codes to classify many diseases and signs, symptoms, complaints, abnormal findings, social circumstances, and various mechanisms of injury or causes of disease. All health conditions can be assigned a unique category and code (up to six characters in length). Categories encompass a set of similar diseases and conditions.
- A significant alternative to the ICD's mental disorders section is the American Psychiatric Association's (APA) Diagnostic and Statistical Manual of Mental Disorders (DSM). In the United States and some other countries, this serves as the primary diagnostic system for psychiatric and psychological disorders, and it is used as a complementary diagnostic system in many other countries.

The Individuals with Disabilities Education Act (IDEA) protects students who are diagnosed as disabled and/or exceptional.

INTERPRETATION AND INSIGHT

The patient (artist), rather than the therapist, should direct the artwork interpretation in effective art therapy. Patients are encouraged to imagine, and then create in art, the emotions and thoughts that they can't verbally express. The artwork product is then reviewed, and patient interprets its meaning. Typically, the artwork analysis enables the patient to gain insight into their feelings and offers a constructive manner to work through their issues.

VERBAL LANGUAGE AND IMAGE

In art therapy sessions, art serves as a form of language, that along with verbal discussion, helps the patient reach a deeper level of self-understanding. Art therapy uses images, art media, the creative process, and reflections from the patient of their development, abilities, personality, concerns, interests, and conflicts. The produced artwork and the corresponding emotions may be reviewed together with the help of the therapist, so that new insights are integrated. Difficult feelings or memories to recall or understand may be explored visually and verbally. Art therapy provides a method of initially nonverbally expressing one's self and then verbally processing the art product.

PSYCHOPHARMACOLOGY

The basic psychopharmacology concepts are as follows:

- Psychopharmacology is the pharmacology branch that addresses the development, actions, and effects of psychoactive drugs. Essentially, psychopharmacology is the study of changes in mood, thinking, and behavior induced by drugs.
- Addiction: A disorder that is progressive, chronic, and relapsing and may include: craving and having a compulsion to use alcohol or other drugs, an inability to effectively control substance use, and a continued use despite negative consequences.
- Conditioning: A behavioral change due to association between events. Evidence shows that learning influences addiction symptoms.
- Dependence: A term commonly used synonymously with addiction; it is the body's physical need for a specific agent
- Self-administration: The voluntary administration of drugs that have rewarding properties.
- Sensitization: An exaggerated response to a drug because of prior exposure to that drug.
- Tolerance: The condition in which an individual must continually increase the drug's dosage in order to maintain its equivalent effectiveness.
- Withdrawal: The set of reactions or behaviors resulting from abrupt drug use cessation when the body has become dependent on the drug.

PSYCHOPHARMACOLOGY CONCEPTS IN THE PRACTICE OF ART THERAPY

Usually, art therapists work as adjunct therapists with other mental health practitioners. Drug or alcohol use often includes sub-cultural symbols and imagery that can be explored and expressed in art therapy. Substance abuse often masks anger, pain, and loneliness feelings. Art provides a method to release these emotions and creative therapies can often be very helpful in the addiction recovery process. They can offer time to get in touch with one's inner self or with a higher power and serve as way of expressing poorly identified or verbalized feelings. By helping the addicted patient connect with his or her more authentic self, the creative therapies can help increase self-esteem and offer an opportunity to create new experiences beyond painful or habitual emotional patterns. The expressive arts foster a renewed ability for the client to relax without substance dependence.

MANIFESTATION OF ADVERSE DRUG REACTIONS IN ART THERAPY

Drugs and alcohol can significantly alter emotions. With a belligerent or threatening patient or one who appears to be intoxicated, the key concerns should be for safety of the patient, other patients, and staff. Staff should be prepared and trained to handle patients that are belligerent and threatening, and contingencies should be considered in advance regarding containing the individual. At times, it may be necessary to involve law enforcement agencies to address and handle a potentially violent incident. The initial treatment contract should mandate that a patient must arrive in a drug-free state. Otherwise, the patient will not be permitted to participate in sessions.

EFFECTS OF MEDICATION ON THE CREATION OF ARTWORK

The popularity of prescription drugs for treating of a wide range of emotional disorders has risen. When combined with art or other psychotherapies forms, treatment may be more effective. For a patient who is too depressed to actively participate in art therapy, the proper medication can help improve symptoms so that the individual can better respond in therapy. Because medications are often the primary symptom treatment for certain mental disorders, the therapist should closely monitor the patient for side effects, such as dry mouth, sedation, impaired focus, and dizziness.

Art Therapy Assessment

FREE ART EVALUATION

The goal of a free-art evaluation is to encourage the patient to let go of conscious controls and thoughts and be as free as possible with their self-expression. This evaluation type is especially useful for patients who have difficulty verbalizing their feelings and is generally used in the early art therapy sessions. In free-drawing, the patient is responsible for all choices such as:

- Selecting materials and medium type (paint, pastels, clay, etc.)
- Using materials however they choose
- Choosing the subject matter of focus

Free art, according to many art therapists, increases understanding of a patient's developmental level, psychological framework, and emotional status.

ADVANTAGES AND DISADVANTAGES

In a free-art evaluation, patients express their feelings however they wish with limited structure. They are asked to freely express themselves and not to concern themselves with planning the picture. At the end of free-drawing, patients are often asked to share and explain their drawing.

DISADVANTAGES OF FREE-ART:
- Time-consuming
- Brings out details
- Caution must be exercised in interpretation. Drawings may be imitations, wishes, or fantasies that do not always reflect reality.
- Lacks scientific rigor

ADVANTAGES OF FREE-ART:
- Created images often mirror the patient's present problems
- Ideal exercise for patients who have experienced a trauma
- Nonverbal patients are more likely to freely express themselves

STRUCTURED ART EVALUATION

Suggestions and directives in art therapy are an integral part of patient diagnosis and treatment. In art tasks and directives that are structured, the therapist specifies themes or subject matter to elicit responses from the patient. Specific themes are selected to evoke the patient's thoughts on important issues. The therapist chooses certain materials for the patient to use to address specific clinical needs and issues. Directives may be general and simple or specific and complex. The therapist's orientation dictates the language and the level of structure for the art therapy.

ADVANTAGES AND DISADVANTAGES

In a structured art evaluation, the therapist tasks the patient to draw something particular like stick figures or other simple items. The therapist may also choose the media and sequence.

DISADVANTAGES OF STRUCTURED ART:

- Drawings may not necessarily reflect reality
- To be valid and reliable, it must be administered as a battery
- Information obtained is difficult to quantify

ADVANTAGES OF STRUCTURED ART:

- It is an efficient assessment format, for example, Human Figure Drawing Test
- Easily fits within a structured framework, such as problem-solving or cognitive models.
- Can help assess family dynamics and effects of medications
- May help predict dangerous behaviors

PROJECTIVE DRAWING

Projective drawing exercises are based on the assumption that all people "project" their personal needs, feelings, and thoughts. The assessment may also include a test with visual stimuli (like the Rorschach inkblots) or a task creating something structured or unstructured with art materials. Such drawings can provide insight about possible developmental delays and perceptual-motor difficulties while building rapport and encouraging narrative accounts. The following are uses of Projective drawings:

- Determining a patient's functional level
- Formulating treatment goals
- Assessing a patient's strengths
- Gaining a deeper level of understanding of a patient's problems
- Evaluating progress

DIAGNOSTIC DRAWING SERIES

The Diagnostic Drawing Series is a useful art therapy technique for a host of major psychiatric disorders. It is done in three parts. First, the patient is asked to use colored chalk pastels to draw a picture in a 18x24 inch piece of paper. Next, they draw a tree, and lastly, they use lines, shapes, and colors to show how they are feeling. The pictures are interpreted together based on a combination of many factors, including use of color, degree of blending, and the placement on the paper of images and space. The Diagnostic Drawing Series (DDS) is specifically designed for adults, while the Child Diagnostic Drawing Series (CDDS) is specifically designed for children.

These assessments require trained and skilled administrators who are knowledgeable with both the tests' theory and structure. Caution should be

Copyright © Mometrix Media. You have been licensed one copy of this document for personal use only. Any other reproduction or redistribution is strictly prohibited. All rights reserved. This content is provided for test preparation purposes only and does not imply an endorsement by Mometrix of any particular political, scientific, or religious point of view.

exercised with interpretation and these tests may be part of a more comprehensive test battery.

ASSESSMENT TASKS

Art therapy assessment sessions often include the following exploration tasks:

- *Automatic drawing (Scribble Technique)* -- The patient is asked to first relax and then draw scribbles or free lines on paper, which provides the patient the opportunity to let down guards and share more openly with the art therapist.
- *Free Drawing* – The patient is in charge of all choices and is simply told to express themselves freely, without worrying about planning the picture. This technique is helpful because the images created by the patient often mirror their present problems, strengths, weaknesses, and fears. Usually, the patient is asked to explain their drawing.
- *Drawing Completion* -- A patient is given one or more papers with pre-drawn lines or shapes that act as a starting point for them to incorporate into their larger picture. This technique works particularly well for a group discussion.

HOUSE-TREE-PERSON

In 1948, Buck created the House-Tree-Person (HTP) test, which provides a useful measure of attitudes and self-perception in its requirements that the test taker draw a house, tree, and person. The house drawing is intended to provide insight into the test taker's feelings toward their family. The tree drawing is intended to elicit feelings of weakness or strength. The person drawing provides insight into the test taker's self-concept. The HTP test is an appropriate assessment for those over the age of three. Many forensic evaluators use this technique as a component of their clinical interview, particularly with young children, to generate hypotheses that are then validated by other methods.

KINETIC FAMILY DRAWING

In 1970, Burns and Kaufman developed the Kinetic Family Drawing (KFD) technique, which requires the individual taking the test to draw a picture of their entire family. Children are to draw include themselves in their family picture and show the group "doing something." This drawing is intended to indicate the child's attitudes toward their family and capture the overall family dynamics. Sometimes, the KFD is interpreted as part of a child abuse evaluation.

In 1974, Prout and Philips developed the Kinetic School Drawing (KSD) technique, which requires the child to draw a self-portrait, one or more classmates, and a teacher. This drawing is meant to provide insight into the child's attitudes toward school people and their level of school environment function.

THE STANDARD BENDER VISUAL MOTOR GESTALT

This test assesses "visual-motor maturity," and screens for developmental disorders, neurological dysfunction, or brain damage. It is administered to those over the age of three, individually or in a group setting.

BRIDGE DRAWING ASSESSMENT

This is a sequential drawing in which the patient draws a visual representation of the issue, the means of solving it, and the desired solution.

LANDGARTEN PHOTO COLLAGE ASSESSMENT

This is a four-task test that readily adapts to patients of ethnic backgrounds because various cultural images are available. Patients can easily produce this task, even if they are fairly uncomfortable drawing, painting, or sculpting images.

LEVICK EMOTIONAL AND COGNITIVE ART THERAPY ASSESSMENT

This is a test developed for exceptional nonverbal children with the ability to draw. The assessment addresses coping and thinking styles, planning and sequencing, and organization and use of space.

CONFLICTED MATERIAL

Artwork allows patients to nonverbally express issues before they are prepared to discuss the issues verbally with others. The patient may be flooded with lots of unsettling or conflicting material during therapy. Artwork provides the therapist with an opportunity to help the patient process and reconcile the stimuli that therapy elicits.

CLIENT'S ANALYSIS

Although a therapist may offer critical guidance for art exercises, in effective art therapy, the patient, rather than the therapist, should direct the art interpretation. The artwork "analysis" usually allows patients to gain insight into their thoughts and feelings and work through issues constructively.

INFLUENCES ON ARTWORK

Art techniques and materials should be appropriate for the patient's age and ability. Depending on their level of function, people with impairments, like a neurological condition or a traumatic brain injury, may struggle with the self-discovery part of the art therapy process.

Art therapy can be an especially useful treatment technique for children with limited language skills. It is also frequently prescribed for chronically and terminally ill individuals as an adjunct to pain control therapy. Art therapy is also used with traditional medical techniques to treat organic conditions and diseases, such as Alzheimer's disease.

CONSCIOUS AND UNCONSCIOUS

Consciousness refers generally to one's state of alertness and awareness of their environment. Unconsciousness means that the individual is not able to be aware of their present surroundings. Jung considered symbols, which is anything used to represent something else, to be the language of the unconscious. Example symbols include a sound, mandalas, lines on paper, crosses, signs, mathematics formulas, words, letters, and even gestures.

When images emerge from the unconscious mind, they bear a significant amount of psychic information. The goal should not be to accurately decipher what is within the image, but rather to ask concise questions about what it may be communicating. For an individual to learn from his or her unconscious, he or she needs to be aware of its contents and suggestions. Spontaneous drawings and paintings serve as an effective way to gain that knowledge.

SYMBOLISM

There are meanings behind various depictions of figures:

- Small figures are interpreted as timid, while large figures represent aggression.
- The dimension of color can also be analyzed with the "House, Tree, Person" activity. The average exercise result uses five colors, but an inhibited person may rely on only a single marker or crayon and a more psychotic person may use many.

Strict interpretations of figures and colors are controversial because they often do not consider the patient's socioeconomic class, culture, and individuality. When interpreting artwork in therapy sessions, therapists need to consider these variables. Interpretation can often be challenging because a psychotic person's messages will reflect their complex thinking.

ART AS TRANSFERENCE

Transference is when the patient unconsciously projects their feelings onto their therapist. It has been a subject of debate in art therapy for years because such therapy provides unique transference circumstances.

Margaret Naumburg was a proponent of the concept of transference and she argued that it occurred in both art and verbal exchange. She held the idea that the picture maker developed an emotional connection to both the therapist and to the art expression. Additionally, she believed that patients' attachment to the artwork they created gradually supplanted their dependence on their therapist. Moreover, she felt that by avoiding interpretation, the therapist could encourage this autonomy. Most therapists agree that some level of transference is always present due to art expression's projective nature and the relationship between patient and therapist.

DIALOGUING WITH AN IMAGE

According to Jung's definition, consciousness refers to perception of a relationship between one's ego and another entity that is either part of the individual's inner world or outside of it. Dialoguing is one method of processing experience. Patients often find it difficult to separate themselves from a feeling. If a patient is struggling with dialoguing, it is often helpful to add an imaginary image, so long as it comes from the patient's own imaginations. Otherwise, he or she will not respect the dialogue's "legitimacy". These dialogues can serve as mirrors for visualizing aspects of one's personality and experiences with a more objective viewpoint.

MENTAL STATUS EXAM

The mental status examination (MSE) assesses the patient's current (in the moment) cognitive ability level, emotional mood, appearance, and speech or thought patterns. The MSE is one component of a full neurological examination, which also includes the examiner's observations of the patient's attitude, answers, and cooperativeness. The MSE measures cognitive functions such as the patient's sense of time, place, and self-identity, as well as his or her memory, general intellectual level, speech, mathematical ability, judgment or insight, and problem-solving or reasoning ability. The MSE is an integral of the differential diagnosis of dementia as well as a host of other psychiatric symptoms and disorders. A MSE is inappropriate for a patient who is unable to pay attention to the examiner, such as those who are unconscious or in a coma, or those with aphasia or lack fluency in the MSE's language of administration.

THE TEN AREAS OF FUNCTIONING IN THE MENTAL STATUS EXAMINATION (MSE)

- *Appearance* -- Patient's age, race, sex, overall appearance, and civil status.
- *Movement and behavior* -- Patient's gait, posture, facial expression, coordination, eye contact, and facial expressions.
- *Affect* -- Outwardly apparent or observable emotions and attitudes.
- *Mood* – Patient's underlying emotional "atmosphere" or tone.
- *Speech* – Patient's speech volume, speed, and length, appropriateness, and clarity of responses.
- *Thought content* -- Indications from responses of delusions, hallucinations, obsessions, dissociation symptoms, or thoughts of suicide. Dissociation is the cutting off of certain mental processes or memories from conscious awareness. Dissociative symptoms include depersonalization feelings and confusion about self-identity and reality.
- *Thought process* - Repeated words and phrases, irrelevant details, interrupted thinking, and confusing or illogical connections between stated thoughts.
- *Cognition* - Knowing one's orientation with regard to personal identity, time, and place.
- *Judgment* –How one would handle or address a commonsense problem.
- *Insight* – One's ability to recognize an issue and understand its severity and nature.

TERMS IN THE MENTAL STATUS EXAMINATION

BEHAVIOR

- *Psychomotor agitation* -- Noticeable increase in body movements, such as hand wringing, pacing, or marked fidgeting
- *Psychomotor retardation* – Noticeable slowing of body movements and speech, lack of usual fidgetiness and movement

MOOD

- Expansive – Enthusiastic and energetic
- *Euphoric* – Gleeful as if having just won the lottery

AFFECT

- *Blunted* – Decreased or muted emotional expression
- *Flat* -- Virtually no affective expression
- *Constricted* -- Restricted range of emotional expression but normal amplitude
- *Inappropriate* -- Expressed emotions are not matched with the patient's thoughts
- *Labile* -- Unpredictable emotional status shifts

THOUGHT PROCESS

- *Circumstantial* -- Organized but overly inclusive
- *Tangential* -- Occasional organization lapses
- *Loosening of associations* -- Lapses in connection between thoughts that frequently occur
- *Blocking* -- Loses in train of thought
- *Neologisms* – Patient-created words with their own idiosyncratic meanings
- *Flight of ideas* -- Extremely rapid flow of thoughts with intact connections

THOUGHT CONTENT

- *Delusion* -- A false belief firmly held by the patient but not shared by their culture.
- *Obsession* -- An intrusive and ego-dystonic idea
- *Overvalued idea* -- A delusion that is not fixed
- *Paranoid ideation* – Undue suspiciousness about the motives and ideas of reference held by others
- *Phobia* -- A specific fear that causes situational or object avoidance despite the patient's understanding that their fear is irrational

CONCEPTS OF PERCEPTIONS

- *Illusion* – Misinterpreted sensory stimulus from any sensory modality (e.g. incorrectly perceiving that the billowing curtains in a dark room is an intruder)
- *Hallucination* -- Perceiving a sight, sound, touch, taste, or smell in the absence of any external sensory stimulation in a degree that is indistinguishable from the same experience would be in reality
- *Depersonalization* – One's sense that they are outside of themselves
- *Derealization* -- A vague unrealistic perception of the external world

OBJECTIVES OF INTERVIEWING

Behavioral interviewing is based on the premise that past behavior quite accurately predicts future performance. Behavioral interview questions frequently begin with one of the following:

- "Tell me about ..."
- "Describe a time when ..."
- "What happened when you ..."

The interview process has three primary objectives:

- To form a respectful, therapeutic relationship by providing dignity to the patient via nonjudgmental, supportive concern
- To assess the patient's needs and form a plan for satisfying those needs
- To motivate and educate the patient to make behavior changes that improve overall well-being

CREATING AN ATMOSPHERE

To best facilitate the information transfer from the patient to the interviewer, the person interviewing needs to create an environment of reassurance and support. The following techniques can facilitate this process:

- Attending -- The interviewer should remain aware of the patient's verbal and nonverbal communication
- Questions -- Asking about the patient's past incidents helps assess their situation.
- Encouraging Responses -- During the interview process, the patient needs confirmation that the interviewer is paying attention, listening, and providing encouragement.
- Nonverbal Communications -- The interviewer should inset periods of silence to give the patient time to respond in a natural way.
- Normalization -- The interviewer should make affirmative and encouraging statements for the comfort of the client
- Balance Statements -- The interviewer should provide the patient with a host of possible emotions in a way that the patient can affirm or respond
- Clarification -- the interviewer can ask the patient to explain a feeling or statement
- Paraphrasing -- The interviewer should restate the content of the patient's statement in their own words
- Providing Words for Feelings -- The interviewer should ask the patient to verbally respond about their emotional experience
- Empathy vs. Sympathy - Sympathy results when the interviewer becomes overly involved with the patient by attempting to experience the patient's feelings. Empathy should be the goal, rather than sympathy, as the interviewer can recognize the patient's situation while avoiding excessive attachment
- Assess Understanding -- The interviewer should regularly ensure that the patient understands everything occurring during the interview
- Summarization -- The interviewer should provide a recap of what has been shared during the interview together.

Important considerations for the interviewer to establish a respectful, comfortable environment for the patient include:

- Dress -- The interviewer should don professional attire
- Consultation Room -- A private interviewing room in relaxed setting is needed
- Greeting -- The interviewer should introvert themselves and personally request the patient from the waiting space.
- Seating -- Patients should be given the most comfort seating option
- Introductions -- The interviewer should introduce themselves and ask what the patient would like to be called as well as what they believe will occur during the interview.
- Setting the Rules -- The interviewer should ensure that the patient understands the interview confidentiality and the allowances for sharing interview information
- Visit schedule -- It is important to discuss the frequency of interviews and any involvement of other people
- Termination/Closure Ritual of the interview session -- There should be an established routine for bringing interviews to a close

Art Therapy Theory and Application

PRINZHORN COLLECTION

The Prinzhorn Collection of the Art of the Mentally Ill includes drawings, paintings, and sculptures created by institutionalized mental patients of mostly German-speaking backgrounds between 1880 and 1920. Prinzhorn felt there was a link between the works made by those with mentally illness and advanced art. Furthermore, he believed art creation could lead to the "primary experience" that those with mental illness seemed naturally able to tap into. As different as the collection's works are in style, they still share certain characteristics; for example, they are not self-conscious, the images did not undergo a planning or verbalization process before production, they lack a systematic approach to space or there is no space at all, and the works rarely expand or open up. In 1921, when Prinzhorn published Expressions of Insanity, the collection gained widespread popularity. It influenced many European artists between the two World Wars and various American artists after 1945.

UNCONSCIOUS INFLUENCES ON ART

Sigmund Freud's discovery and description of the unconscious sparked an art and culture revolution in the early 20th century. Freud developed the theory that unconscious motives control many behaviors. He believed that artists had special insight ability into psychic truth. This spurred artists to discover a whole world of the subconscious to explore through dreams, irrationality, and alternate reality. Freud's theories provided artists with many new themes and influenced surrealism, which explores the unconscious mind's inner depths. Freud believed that one's unconscious is the source of their motivations, from the simple desires for food or sex to the more complex motives of an artist. These motivations are often only available to the individual in disguised form.

CONCEPT OF SYMBOLS

Jung developed his own systematic theories under the umbrella of analytical psychology. His most notable concepts are archetypes and the collective unconscious. Jung believed the unconscious mind primarily expresses itself through symbols. Jung encouraged his patients to sculpt, paint, or use some other art form to explore their inner depths. His influence on art therapy stemmed from his interest in artwork's inherent psychological meaning, especially that in the mandala. Also influential was his fascination with his own drawings as well as those of his patients.

OTTO RANK

Otto Rank was formally a follower of Freud. He developed a psychotherapy style that focused on real relationships in the here-and-now, the conscious mind, and one's will, rather than past history, transference, wishes, and the unconscious. He was interested in art and education. Rank described three basic types of persons that humans can become: productive, adapted, or neurotic. The productive is the artist, genius, creative, and self-conscious type of person who accepts and affirms

69

themselves and creates an ideal that functions as a positive focus for their will. As a therapist, Rank attempted to shorten the time required psychoanalysis to be successful to just a few months.

PROJECTIVE TECHNIQUES OF ASSESSMENT

Projective assessment techniques access buried information by helping the patient to project it elsewhere. The basic premise is to provide stimuli that are neutral and non-threatening to a patient and then ask them to interpret ambiguous pictures, make associations, fill in the blanks, or tell stories. According to projection theory, patients project their unconscious impulses onto the various non-threatening stimuli, which allows the evaluator to interpret and guide the patient toward increased insight. The recommendation of most psychologists is to use projective techniques in conjunction with other assessments.

Some traditional assessment techniques include:

- Rorschach Inkblot Test
- Thematic Apperception Test (TAT)
- House-Tree-Person
- Free Association
- Dream Analysis
- Word Association
- Sentence Completion

DEVELOPMENT OF ART THERAPY

The sociological and intellectual developments in the late 19th and early 20th century largely influenced art therapy theory and practice development, as during this time, psychiatrists became interested in the artwork their patients with mental illness created. Art therapy as a profession in the United States emerged around the 1940s as a result of Margaret Naumburg's work with children's art. Two art therapy approaches emerged during the 1970s. Practitioners who exercised the "art as therapy" approach emphasized the innate healing power of creating art itself. Therapists who considered themselves to have an "art psychotherapy" practice used art as a healing technique within the verbal psychotherapy format. The 1970s and 1980s were formative years in the art therapy profession. Medicine and psychiatry partnerships resulted in creating jobs in mental health or medical centers, substance abuse programs, and day treatment programs.

ART THERAPY INFLUENCERS

The development of art therapy was influenced by the following historic figures:

- Margaret Naumburg: She defined the art-in-therapy theory. The emphasis on Naumburg's is on making the unconscious become conscious, free association, spontaneous drawing, and interpretation.

- Edith Kramer: She proposed the approach of art-as-therapy as being process-oriented. She said, "Goals of art as therapy are to support the ego, foster the development of identity, and promote maturation." In her thoughts, the counselor should function more as a facilitator.
- Elinor Ulman: She is credited with starting the first academic journal in the field. With her friend Bernard Levy, she initiated an early training program.
- Hanna Kwiatkowska: She worked with the National Institute of Mental Health to develop a way of integrating art and therapy and developed the Family Art Evaluation, which is a structural evaluation method for families.
- Florence Crane: She was an art educator that believed art itself was therapy instead of just a means for therapy. She modified art education principles to use with children. She emphasized free artistic expression, scribbling, and movement.

EDITH KRAMER

Kramer began her working career in a hospital but left to study psychoanalysis. She believed that art therapy was a useful method of integrating conflicts aesthetically so as to balance the id, ego, and superego. In her art therapy work with children, Kramer blended in Freudian personality theory, and emphasized the importance of Freudian defense mechanisms like sublimation. Through the sublimation experience, Kramer believed that content and form synthesis was achieved via transforming emotional material and thoughts into fully formed images. Kramer believed that act of creating art itself is therapeutic, while others argued that art is simply a means for the therapist and patient to meet on common ground.

MARGARET NAUMBURG

Naumburg felt that art had symbolic qualities derived from the subconscious mind. She subscribed to free association, a Freudian concept. Naumburg encouraged the patient to verbally describe spontaneous art. She did not select a specific theory for interpreting patients' artwork and suggested that their created free associations were critical to understanding images created during therapy and would often lead to change and personal growth.

THERAPY AND PSYCHOTHERAPY

Art as therapy, a concept introduced by Edith Kramer, is a product-oriented approach in which the primary focus is art expression for academic, cultural, or aesthetic aims. Therapists who employ this approach believe that the patient, through the creative process, can better reconcile their emotional conflicts and increase self-awareness and personal growth.

Margaret Naumberg's *art as psychotherapy* process-oriented approach focuses on both the art product and any associations as a way to assist patients to better reconcile their emotional conflicts and increase self-awareness and personal growth. Therapist who employ this approach view the art creation process, the content, the manner in which the forms are presented, and the verbal associations to the artwork as a reflection of a patient's personality traits, unconscious, and development.

VERBAL COMMUNICATION AND ART THERAPY

Patients share their problems verbally in all major schools of psychotherapy, and the therapy occurs via verbal exchanges between the therapist and patient. Typically, the patient talks and the therapist listens. The patient, therefore, speaks more than the therapist does, and when the therapist does speak in the session, it is about issues already mentioned by the patient.

Art therapy gives patients both verbal and nonverbal outlets, because patients visually present their problems. During the artwork creation process or after completion, usually verbal interaction regarding the artwork with the therapist occurs.

ART THERAPY CONCEPTS

Three important art therapy concepts include:

- Transference -- the tendency of patients to transfer their emotional responses generated in an earlier time towards their therapist. In is generally accepted that transference in some degree is always present. It is important that therapist remain aware of this potential occurrence.
- Art object Permanence -- provides a tangible and more permanent record of thoughts, an opportunity to recall emotions that occurred when the art was initially created, and an opportunity to explore, reexamine, and work through those earlier feelings.
- Externalization -- a therapy approach that encourages the patient to externalize their problems as a way to relieve the self-blame and responsibility. This allows separation of the person and the problem to help therapy focus on solutions. It is particularly useful with patients lacking verbal skills, such as children.

WORLD VIEW REVEALED

Art therapy has applications for a variety of family issues as it provides the opportunity for each family member to see the family as a whole from every member's personal perspective. Therapists delve into how families have constructed social phenomena knowledge, created gender attitudes, taught beliefs, and developed language. Through art therapy, it is possible to identify recurrent interactions and problematic family structures.

Adler first addressed the important relationship between one's self and society at large. He viewed humans as being "capable of profound cooperation in living together and striving for self-improvement, self-fulfillment, and contribution to the common welfare." Adler was one of the first therapists to recognize that a child's birth order position in a family could have a significant impact on the child's development. It is important to feel like a valued member of the family and children may get discouraged if they feel their position in the sibling lineup is disadvantageous.

ART THERAPY AND EDUCATION

Art therapy and art education both teach techniques, employ similar materials, strive to get persons to express their inner feelings and thoughts, and help foster growth. Both aim to help the patient grow. Art therapy employs art as a therapeutic device. The emphasis in art therapy is on the creative process itself. The art therapist is specifically trained and skilled in art therapy techniques and different interventions. Art education focuses specifically on the techniques used to create the finished artwork product. The two differ in that the focus of art therapy is to use the feelings and behaviors being expressed as a means of assessing the nature of the conflict and determine the best way to help the patient cope with the problems.

ROLE OF ART PRODUCT

The artwork produced can be used for communication, associations, and diagnostic purposes as it is an extension of the patient. It frequently mirrors the patient's defense mechanisms, inner conflicts, and developmental issues. It provides a safe framework for the patient to explore and experience the world around them. It provides a tool for the therapist that permits patient-therapist communication that enables the patient to resolve their inner conflicts and heal. The created artwork serves a focus for verbal reflection between the patient and the therapist and as a tangible reference point to assess progress.

USEFUL TECHNIQUES

To best help patients express their feelings, solve problems, develop social skills, resolve emotional problems, or reduce anxiety, special art therapy techniques that often particularly useful include the following:

- The Scribble technique is helpful for the patient who "feels stuck."
- "Direct" drawing exercises can help decrease group resistance in crises by introducing exercises that may reduce the patient's need to verbally explain their crisis.
- Collages allow patients to select a picture that relates to an emotion that best expresses how the patient felt when the event happened. They can also breakdown barriers.
- Unstructured drawing activities allow patients to select and use various media in whatever way they choose.
- Free-drawing, finger painting, and mask-making help nonverbal patients express regrets, perform life review, resolve unresolved losses, and address issues, such as grief, aging, and fear of dying.

CONCERN FOR AESTHETICS

The produced artwork need not be aesthetically pleasing for effective art therapy. Rather, it must express feelings to gain insight into emotions and thoughts. The therapist should remain non-judgmental so that the patient can express and release their feelings and thoughts and develop a greater sense of self-awareness. The patient will use the process of creating art to organize and make sense of confusing and misunderstood feelings. The resulting artwork will capture the process that the patient endured. It will not be created for an aesthetically pleasing purpose.

USE OF LANGUAGE

Art therapy encourages individuals to use art to express and understand their emotions. A crucial feature of art therapy effectiveness is that the patient, rather than the therapist, should direct the artwork interpretation. Verbal and nonverbal communication can further help the patient express or explain the thoughts or feelings behind the artwork, the manner of which depends on the patient's willingness and ability to speak openly about their artwork. Sometimes the verbal communication about one's piece of artwork is therapeutic itself.

TEACHING TECHNIQUE CONSIDERATIONS

The art therapist's specific techniques utilized with a patient depend on several factors such as:

- The art therapist's theoretical background
- The art therapist's knowledge of specific art techniques and media
- The therapy goals, which are derived from the assessment process
- The treatment plan for the patient
- The therapy setting (outpatient, inpatient)
- The patient's demographics (age, mental ability, culture) and their functional implications
- The therapist's chosen approach (direct, non-direct)

IMPORTANCE OF ACCEPTANCE

The art therapist needs to convey an attitude of unconditional positive regard for the patient and his or her artwork in order for the patient to overcome anxieties and freely express their inner feelings and thoughts. Patients need to feel that they can express their fears and insecurities in an accepting relationship context. This helps to alleviate some of the experienced anxieties, which can result in reframing or expressing things differently. The art therapist should not critique the artwork; they should just help the patient talk about it.

ROLE OF ART MATERIALS

Various art materials and techniques are designed to help the patient connect with their inner feelings, fantasies, and desires by creating visual representations of them, with the goal that the patient will become increasingly self-aware. Then, the art therapist will attempt to help the patient process these feelings and move toward a solution or a healthier coping mechanism. Artwork created by patients may also trigger the defense mechanism of regression, which occurs when a patient copes with unacceptable, unpleasant, or unwanted feelings or thoughts by reverting to earlier, more primitive ways of thinking and acting.

LIFE REPRESENTED SYMBOLICALLY

Art therapy is founded on the belief that the process or act of creating art is an embodied action that concretely and/or symbolically reflects the patient's experience of existing, which includes conscious and unconscious conflicts. Art brings visibility to difficult or painful things to see or verbalize. Using art materials opens opportunities for patients to gain awareness of thinking and feeling anomalies and to generate more options for viewing, understanding, and clarifying their feelings, beliefs and life events. In making art, conflict, trauma, or fear is re-experienced, integrated, and resolved.

BENEFITS OF ART THERAPY

The creating of art in itself is a therapeutic and healing process, during which expression of conflicts, feelings, and fantasies can relieve tension, evoke new emotions, promote self-knowledge, offer sensory stimulation, and increase awareness and possible acceptance of the realized feelings, conflicts, and fantasies expressed. The created picture becomes a basis for self-exploration and self-understanding. The art making process and the finished artwork product facilitates discussion regarding some of the patient's issues. The patient is able, through artwork, to represent a feeling or thought to make it tangible and concrete.

CONVEYING MEANING THROUGH ART

Art elements themselves like lines, shapes, forms, textures, spaces, values, compositions, colors, and perspectives lend meaning to the art. The art elements enable the patient to effectively communicate complex feelings and ideas using a common language. An art therapist should not analyze or interpret the client's artwork, but should allow the patient to tell the artwork's story. The therapist may have responses, ideas, or questions about the patient's artwork, but ultimately, the therapist does not know the meaning of the produced work beyond what the patient verbally shares. The therapist is most interested in the elements of a produced artwork because they frequently reveal information about the patient's thought processes. Some variables involved in drawing can be assessed using the Formal Elements Art Therapy Scale (FEATS).

CONVEYING FEELING THROUGH ART

An art piece can be viewed compositionally in terms of its relationships between the figure and ground, the quality and completeness of the piece's forms, and the internal components' relationships to each other. Most colors carry personal, cultural, expressive, and emotional implications. Vertical and horizontal elements like lines and shapes possess a feeling of order and calm, while diagonals are more inherently dynamic and suggest movement. Artwork attains a more dynamic appearance by varying the values, which also lends a hierarchy among the figures and causes some to stand out and others to recede. Visual balance causes the elements to feel as though they have been arranged well, but imbalances cause uneasiness.

KNOWING PRINCIPLES HELPS IN UNDERSTANDING

Knowing art's formal elements and principles allows the therapist to appropriately appreciate, analyze, and discuss the patient's artwork. All artwork has some sort or order determined by its artist: swirling and dynamic, balanced and symmetrical, or chaotic and even seemingly random. Rough brushstrokes or clashing colors tend to convey violent emotions, like anger or anguish. Subdued colors and gentle curves tend to elicit quieter and peaceful emotions. Although it is common to assume that the patient expresses the emotions experienced while creating the artwork, but more often, patients choose an appropriate expressive style for the artwork's subject matter, genre, or setting. For example, small figures drawn are interpreted as timid, while large figures drawn represent aggression. Drawings often reveal the relationships between the patient's family members.

METAPHORS AND SYMBOLS

METAPHORS

A metaphor is a direct comparison between two or more subjects that are seemingly unrelated. A metaphor presents one subject or item as being equal or closely related to another in some way. The patient's thoughts and feelings are often concealed or disguised, but artwork is a way to expresses them metaphorically. The patient can put their thoughts and feelings into the artwork images, which allows the art therapist an avenue to discuss the image's metaphor.

For example, if a child feels uncomfortable or unable to talk openly about problem, the art therapist may ask him or her to draw a picture that demonstrates what happened to a stuffed animal instead. The drawing often ends up telling the story behind the child's injury.

SYMBOLS

Symbols often appear the patient's sculptures, drawings, or paintings, but they are not necessarily universal between patients. All symbols and their associations are unique to the patient and influenced by their history, personal circumstances, culture, and therapy stage. Most therapists do not attempt to interpret the symbols' meanings. Some art therapists use the generated symbols to guide the conversation, while bringing in unconscious information to the immediate situation. Other therapists will only discuss what the patient thinks and feels about their artwork, while others remain quiet and allow the patient to explore what they have made. Symbols drawn repeatedly by the patient in the same way are called stereotyped art.

IMPORTANCE OF SYMBOLIC METAPHOR IN ARTWORK AND THE ART PROCESS

Symbols and metaphors serve as vehicles for communicating and expressing powerful thoughts and feelings. Art therapy often uses symbolic metaphor as a diagnostic tool. For example, missing or distorted body parts in images, or houses expelling fire or smoke can be important signals to art therapists, indicative of problems such as depression, abuse, or anger.

If a patient feels uncomfortable discussing what is causing his or her issues, he or she can often communicate this information metaphorically. Art's use of metaphor allows the patient to focus on a pictorial image that symbolically represents their experience. By focusing on the symbol, the patient is able to express their feelings without having to directly refer to specific details of their traumatic or difficult experience.

CONSCIOUS, UNCONSCIOUS, OR PRECONSCIOUS MEANING IN ART

Freud was the first to introduce the idea that the human mind is made of three individual layers or areas:

- Conscious: the mind's smallest part, which inhabits the uppermost layer.
- Preconscious: the mind's deeper part that the individual cannot reach, except through their dreams.
- Unconscious: the mind's largest area, which Freud considered the reservoir for painful memories.

The patient, through art therapy, is able to connect with unconscious symbolic language and bring out visual material that increases one's self-awareness more effectively. Images resembling memories allow feelings to surface and permit the disclosure of important assessment information, which can help the therapist form a treatment plan.

TRANSFERENCE COMMUNICATION BETWEEN CLIENT AND THERAPIST AS MUTUAL SYMBOLIC LANGUAGE

Transference is the projection of the client's unconscious feelings onto the therapist. The first time a patient meets his or her new therapist, transference begins, although it can even begin before that, pre-treatment, as the patient imagines what his or her therapist will be like.

In art therapy, transference of at least some degree exists due to the following two factors:

- Art expression's projective nature
- The therapist and patient's relationship

The therapist needs to be aware of the potential harms of the therapeutic relationship that can cause ethical issues and ultimately inhibit the healing process.

LEVELS OF MEANING, EXPRESSION, AND EXPERIENCE IN ARTWORK AND THE ART THERAPY PROCESS

Artwork integrates a patient's inner perceptions and experiences with his or her outside world experiences. It reflects the patient's relationships to other people, the environment, and general society. Additionally, the patient's art expression is affected by his or her cognitive abilities, developmental maturity, emotional development, spirituality, and interpersonal skills. Although artistic expressions may share various commonalities in content, style, and form, the art therapist must allow for the patient's personal art expressions to take on a host of meanings and avoid using therapeutic approaches that strictly categorize images or assign predetermined meanings for image content. The art therapist needs to be open to multiple meanings to fully understand and appreciate the specific meaning being conveyed.

CREATIVITY AND MENTAL HEALTH

Creativity is frequently used as a mental health indicator. Creativity's relation to mental wellness as a concept may be supported by research concerning the creative process' therapeutic value. There have been numerous studies that have indicated that therapeutic effectiveness of the creative arts for patients suffering from mental illness. The therapy is believed to act as a means of releasing trapped emotions. Studies also indicate that there is a connection between one's creative ability and their risk of developing a mental disorder, such that the prevalence of mental problems in creative people is significantly higher than for that of the general population.

UNCONSCIOUS CONFLICT AND HEALTH

In psychoanalytic theory, the unconscious mind contains repressed desires or memories not subject to conscious control or perception but that can affect every aspect of one's daily functioning. Mental tension is thought to stem from unresolved conflict. The psychotherapist's role is to facilitate the situation in therapy so that the issue emerges from within the patient's own experience in their own unconscious language.

ART MAKING AND HEALTH

It is generally accepted that both art and mental health therapy include flexible problem-solving—a process in which one perceives and resolves a gap between their present situation and intended goal, with the road to the goal impeded by known or unknown obstacles. Typically, the situation is not one that has been previously encountered, or such that a specific solution taken from past experiences is unknown.

The creative process emphasizes self-actualization and problem-solving. It is also generally accepted that both art and mental health therapy include the appropriate expression and management of feelings such as frustration, happiness, fear, anger, sadness, and disappointment. The art therapist must respect the patient's rights to personal freedom, autonomy, choices, and values as they work collaboratively to help the patient find healing.

PRIMARY, SECONDARY, TERTIARY THINKING

Freud was the first to explain levels of thinking processes as the following:

- Primary thinking refers to information (considered "common sense knowledge") that the senses have the ability to perceive. Primary thinking is a common and developmentally normal part of childhood, but rather rare in healthy adults.

78

- Secondary thinking processes are those learned, cultivated, and shaped as the individual develops within their environment and culture. Human personality is comprised of one's processing information modalities and created mental representations. As a person develops, by roughly age 6, secondary process thinking supersedes primary.
- Tertiary process thinking occurs when primary and secondary are integrated. Sylvan Arietta defines creativity itself as the "tertiary process." It occurs when the brain's right and left sides bridge to create a unique thought form.

THEORIES OF CREATIVITY

- Many psychoanalysts believe that creativity stems from unconscious drives and desires to find happiness. Fantasies are imagined to fulfill unsatisfied wishes as well as to escape from an unsatisfactory reality to one of pleasure and devoid of pain. Typically, psychoanalytic theories maintain that creative productivity results from preconscious mental activity.
- Behaviorists believe that creativity results from one's environment and genetic make-up, and that environmental stimuli responses are compiled to yield creative behavior. To encourage creative behavior, an individual must cultivate their environment in a way that allows creativity to flow.
- The cognitive approach believes creativity is a thinking process or learned behavior that can be improved with practice. Cognitive theorists believe that creativity grows from a capacity to make new and unusual mental associations between concepts.

TRANSFERENCE COMMUNICATION BETWEEN CLIENT AND THERAPIST AS MUTUAL SYMBOLIC LANGUAGE

Transference is the projection of the client's unconscious feelings onto the therapist. The first time that a patient meets his or her therapist, transference begins, but it can even start before the first meeting when the patient imagines what his or her therapist will be like.

Some degree of transference occurs in art therapy for two reasons:

- Art expression's projective nature
- The nature of the patient-therapist

The therapist should be aware of the potential harm inherent in the therapeutic relationship, which can cause ethical issues and inhibit the patient's healing process.

LEVELS OF MEANING, EXPRESSION, AND EXPERIENCE IN ARTWORK AND THE ART THERAPY PROCESS

Artwork integrates the patient's inner perceptions and experiences and his or her experiences of the external world. It reflects the patient's relationships to other people, the environment, and society at large. Additionally, the patient's art expression is affected by his or her emotional development, interpersonal skills, spirituality, developmental maturity, and cognitive abilities. Although art expressions within and between patients may have similar forms, styles, and content, the art therapist needs to allow each patient's artwork to take on a variety of meanings freely without categorizing or assigning predetermined meanings. The art therapist must remain open to multiple of meaning or he or she may misunderstand the individual's intended meanings in each piece.

Recipient Populations

VIKTOR LOWENFELD

Viktor Lowenfeld developed an art development theory that correlates with the child's chronological age. Lowenfeld authored Creative and Mental Growth, a manual that serves as a standard for training art therapists and educators. He allowed children to create their own art and urged teachers to permit students to do what they desired. Lowenfeld described childhood stages of artistic development based on understanding the growth process and named the five developmental stages of the art process: Scribble, Pre-schematic, Schematic, Social/Gang, and Naturalistic. These stages are based on characteristics displayed in the child's art rather than their age.

- The Scribble stage typically ranges from age 2 to 4. The name reflects the child's development of the ability to imagine or visualize in images.
- The Preschematic stage typically ranges from age 4 to 6 and is marked with the emergence of visual ideas or schema. The use of color and space have little meaning and little understanding.
- The Schematic stage typically ranges from age 7 to 9 years and is characterized by natural colors and identifiable shapes.
- The Drawing Realism/gang stage typically ranges from age 9 to 11 and is characterized by more detailed human forms and the appearance of perspective.
- The Pseudorealistic stage typically ranges from
- age 11 to 13 with an important end result. Older children are generally more concerned with whether art resembles what they are drawing or sculpting.

RHODA KELLOGG

Rhoda Kellogg authored Analyzing Children's Art, which described what she learned from directly observing young children's drawing from around the world. Kellogg identified twenty basic scribbles most often used by children. These scribbles are composed of vertical, horizontal, circular, diagonal, curving, and waving dots and lines. She also found that these scribbles manifested in seventeen major patterns and included "archetypal symbols", which are recurring designs.

She stated the following points:

- Children from all cultures, regardless of their differing cultural backgrounds and influences, go through these same five stages of artistic development.
- The developmental stages are predictable and consistent among children.
- These stages are experienced without training, teaching, or coaxing.

She concluded that a child's artistic development is arrested when there is interference with the child's natural, innate ability to draw, which usually occurs when the child starts school and adult expectations of "approved artwork" get superimposed on the child's natural desire to experiment with artistic expression.

APPROPRIATE ART MEDIA

The appropriate art media should be supplied to the child according to the different stages of development:

- A child in the scribble stage may be presented with a large piece of paper, chalk, a fat crayon, markers, and paint, as these encourage physical, expressive, sensory development. The smaller or younger the child, the larger the utensil (crayons) should be. Basic paper folding, line drawing, and clay work should be encouraged.
- A child in the pre-schematic and schematic stage should be provided with plenty of materials and opportunities cut, paste, and arrange items.
- A child in the realistic/gang stage can effectively work with oil pastels, broad tipped felt pens, and pre-cut collage pictures, glue sticks and scissors, and paper of various sizes.
- natural development tends to cease during the pseudorealistic stage unless a conscious decision to improve drawing skills is made. All types of materials should be provided.

The art therapist needs to provide culturally "flexible" media. For example, collage materials need to include images potentially representative of his or her life experience.

Examples include the following:

- A child with excessive energy to release is offered clay or play dough that can be pulled, pushed, pushed, and squeezed.
- An autistic child or one with attention problems may benefit from tactile and process-oriented activities.
- A child with difficulty handling overwhelming feeling may benefit from using constrictive mediums.
- A child can use painting to plan and decide about form and color and take the opportunity to work by themselves.
- Working with sand as a media can be relaxing, and offer an interesting sensory experience because of its unstructured quality. It can also help develop social skills and imagination skills as the child must mix, pour, sift, stir, mold, and measure the sand.
- A hyperactive child may best respond to structured more approaches.
- A child with a learning disability often responds well to three-dimensional materials that allow a very hands-on approach to construction.
- Coloring books often damage children's confidence in their own personal schemata.

GOALS

The goals of art therapy are formed according to each patient's diagnosis, needs, abilities, and interests to move toward healing and growth most effectively. Depending on the goals for therapy, appropriate art media to use may include:

- Drawing scribbles or free lines or incorporating pre-drawn simple shapes and lines into one's larger picture on paper, especially if the goals are to optimize spontaneity and free self-expression and to let go of conscious control and thoughts
- Painting, drawing, or collage making is good for building rapport
- Painting materials are helpful to get in touch with one's inner desires and feelings by making visual representations of them
- Painting and drawing materials are useful for developing an awareness of one's body imaged and personal needs
- Drawing, painting, and collage materials can be useful to see and accept where one fits into the world and handle this realization
- group mural or a water play table can help develop social skills.

ROLE OF ENVIRONMENT

Many theorists think that drawing for young children begins as a normal part of a child's effort to explore, manipulate, seek order, and control themselves in their environment. Other theorists think that the initial act of employing media to draw is not out of curiosity, but rather as a way to imitate what they have observed. When a child is somewhere between 12 and 16 years old, he or she faces a crisis in their artistic development, wherein either they already do or do not have enough encouragement and skill to perpetuate a desire to create art. If criticized, discouraged, or deprived she opportunity to experiment and express with art, the child may stop drawing or participating in visual art activities. Children from low-income homes may lack the resources for art and some cultures may put more emphasis on the importance of arts than others.

INFLUENCE OF ADULTS ON A CHILD'S ARTWORK

There are various ways that adults can encourage a child to create artwork:

- By providing art materials to very young children
- By permitting children to use and experiment with media in unique ways.
- By ensuring that children know that drawings do not have to look like photographs, but rather are each creator's view of their world.
- By teaching children that art is a means of self-expression and that whatever the child chooses to express is perfectly fine.
- By exposing the young child to a variety of visual art to encourage a lifelong appreciation of art
- By responding to the artwork with positive discussion

LIMIT SETTING

Limits are intended to provide the child with physical and emotional safety and security, and protects the therapist's physical well-being, other children in group setting, the room, and the art therapy materials. By clearly communicating limits, all of the child's desires and feelings are unconditionally accepted but not all behaviors are. With appropriate limits in the therapy setting, decision-making, self-responsibility, and self-control are consistently fostered and promoted. Limits allow the therapist to define and target acceptable behaviors. Adults should help children understand the self-expressive nature of art and that whatever the child chooses to express is perfectly fine. Artistic experimentation, risk taking, and developing meaning are intrinsic to creating art, and children can start to understand these concepts via their personal artistic efforts.

MOTIVATION AND SELF- ESTEEM

Young children usually embrace working with different art materials, but older children and adolescent are often intimidated by the creating process and report that they "cannot draw" or are "bad at art." These statements may reflect a self-image or self-esteem problem rather than a true lack of artistic expressive ability. Children's reactions to their own drawings and their self-perception their competence is frequently affected by the attitudes and responses of both peers and adults to their artwork. In order to avoid deterring young talent or damaging the child's self-esteem, adults should praise the child for creating something wonderful and ask the child to describe and explain their drawing. From the child's answer, the adult can praise the artwork in context. To overcome or combat inhibited attitudes, an art therapist can choose topics and subjects that are linked to what is important to the child and attempt another approach.

SIGNS OF TRAUMA

Children of all ages can be traumatized. Traumatized children may communicate their distress verbally, behaviorally, and through their play. They often exhibit behaviors that seem disruptive, out of control, excessively aggressive, or fearful. Traumatized children may become "flooded" with anxious and fearful feelings that can overwhelm their ability to effectively regulate or manage such physical and emotional reactions. Every child who has experienced trauma will have his or her own unique experience and reactions. Some have a severe reaction and exhibit many concerning behaviors, while others display fewer signs of trauma experiences, but their exhibited reactions are still intense and troubling. When a child's reactions align with a specific set of symptoms and behaviors, they may be diagnosed with the consisting of Post-Traumatic Stress Disorder (PTSD).

ROLE OF STEREOTYPICAL IMAGERY

During sessions of art therapy, a child may opt to express safe and familiar symbols that he or she can draw well. Those symbols drawn repeatedly in the same way by a child are called stereotyped art, which Edith Kramer believes children use as an attempt at organization, a defense against "emotional upheaval", a means of warding off chaos, or to repeat previous successes. Naumburg considers stereotyped art as "encouraging regression." Kramer also cautioned that such art "may reaffirm and cement a tendency to hide one's emotions behind an artificial façade."

SEPARATION ANXIETY

Child development and the sequence of parent/child attachment typically proceeds as follows: During the baby's first few months of life, most caregivers can effectively provide comfort. From about 7 - 18 months of age, the baby feels distressed over routine separation from parents, home, and other familiar situations. Children in the toddler and preschool years can be anxious and emotional when separated from a caregiver, but they can be distracted by activities initiated with another caregiver or other peers. By the age of three, separation anxiety usually diminishes as the child begins to see themselves from the point of view of others. Usually by age five, the child outgrows normal separation fears. Separation anxiety may increase at any age or may even return in an older child if there is a change in environment or situation, such as a new baby in the family.

SEPARATION ANXIETY DISORDER

Usually, separation anxiety disorder appears in school age children and represents exaggerated fears that are disproportionate to real situations or issues. It can significantly restrict or interfere with a child's normal activities. Signs and symptoms include the following:

- Extreme, disproportionate distress when separated from loved ones
- Unwillingness to attend school, go on outings, or leave home
- Unrealistic worry about potential harm to one's self or one's loved ones
- Continually seeking safety reassurance for one's self or one's loved ones
- Crying, clinging, tantrums, nausea, or vomiting in anticipation of separation from loved ones
- Reluctance, especially at night, to be alone
- Nightmares about harm and danger to one's self or loved ones
- Symptoms existing for at least four weeks

ADOLESCENTS

Adolescence is the identity formation stage characterized by all of the different ways that adolescents develop: socially, physically, cognitively, morally, and emotionally. Adolescents experience a rapid physical growth spurt and undergo sexual maturation, which is accompanied by higher-level cognitive skill development. Moral reasoning, honesty, integrity, and behaviors that intend to help others emerge. Emotional development, at this stage, involves establishing realistic self-identity in terms of relations and stress and emotional coping. Their social development is related to interactions with peers, family, community members, and school and work environments. During the developmental transitions faced by adolescents, issues regarding peer relationships, personal style, and mood swings may cause more than "normal" levels of anxiety and lead to clinical depression, addictions, eating disorders, and other issues. Group therapy settings can be quite beneficial because adolescents are intimately connected to peer groups.

IDENTITY FORMATION IN ADOLESCENTS

Achieving one's sense of identity is a major developmental task faced during adolescence. Theorists state that identity formation begins in childhood but it becomes a major focus during adolescence. Teenagers identify with those they admire, and they tend to emulate the characteristics of those they hope to be like. Teenagers are also significantly impacted by the values and behaviors of their family. They seek out readily observable behavior or possessions. Young people frequently emulate adult behavior. Rebellious behavior may occur if the desire to be unique supersedes one's desire to fit in. The adolescent's self-image is significantly impacted by the opinion of others. Providing all goes well, somewhere within the adolescent years, these various identifications merge into a more unified and unique whole adolescent.

THE ROLE OF SEXUALITY

The adolescent's physical body begins to take on shape characteristics of his or her sex during puberty. Changing hormonal levels activate the development of some secondary sex characteristics including: pubic and underarm hair growth, increased oil production and sweat gland activity, and acne development. New behaviors, thoughts, and physiological changes that occur can often cause confusion and a sense of feeling out of control of bodily changes. Many adolescents react within the typical range of the cultural stereotypes of sexual changes during this time.

PEER RELATIONSHIPS

A peer group is a small group of relatively close friends of the same or similar age who also tend to share the same activities. Teenagers spend a lot of their time in peer groups. These groups can either serve as a positive or negative support system for the individual. Because the powerful influence of peer relationships during adolescence is stronger than it is any other time, teenagers who feel isolated or disenfranchised may develop a variety of disorders, including depression, addiction, and eating disorders. The common denominator in all of the disorders is that the adolescent often feels isolated and disenfranchised. They seek a feeling of belonging, which can often be provided with group therapy. Peer interaction can be a critically important recovery tool for working with youth.

LIMIT SETTING

Adolescents are often one of the most difficult populations to work with in different therapy settings. Giovacchini wrote that they have a "propensity for creating problems within the treatment setting [including]...their reticence about becoming engaged or their inclination to express themselves through action rather than words and feelings." Thus, the therapist may need to explicitly clarify the rules, define appropriate and inappropriate behaviors, and explain the consequences with their adolescent patients so that the patient understands the intention and purpose of the therapy. The main goal is to ensure the adolescent patient that no behavior or problem is too disturbing to address. Limit setting helps preserve the therapeutic relationship, provide both parties with emotional security and feelings of physical safety, and facilitate the adolescent's opportunities or abilities to learn self-responsibility and self-control.

DYNAMICS OF CONTROL/ RESISTANCE/MOTIVATION

Adolescents tend to be much more reluctant than adults to come to therapy. In counseling, adolescents are often unpredictable, clam up during sessions or evaluations, and raise irrelevant or inappropriate questions, comments, or behaviors. Adolescents who have been abused or traumatized with violence may feel reluctant to talk, especially if they have previously been threatened or instructed not to talk about their experiences, themselves, or their families. The adolescent's cultural background, if one where they taught to politely give short responses to questions and to limit speech and eye contact during interactions with adults in authority may also influence openness to talk as these behaviors and values create resistance to the therapeutic process. For the therapist, this can pose a significant challenge to motivating the adolescent patient to express their innermost thoughts and feelings.

SEPARATION-INDIVIDUATION

The processes of separation and individuation are both normal and healthy human development psychological phases that begin in one' first year of life and then continue through childhood, adolescence, and adulthood. Separation leads to independence, personal autonomy, assertiveness, and one's ability to make choices. Individualization creates each person's unique identity, interests, point of view, interests, and likes and dislikes. Adolescents have a need to discover and form their own independence that is from their parents or family members, develop the self-confidence to make decisions, and handle or cope with life stressors themselves. This stage of development is often characterized by challenging authority, rejecting the parents' belief system, and an increasing importance of peer-group identity, all of which may result in conflict.

TRAUMATIC EVENTS

Traumatic events are generally unexpected and uncontrollable, and they likely overwhelm a person's sense of safety and leave them feeling insecure and vulnerable in their environment. There are four general categories of traumatic experience responses:

- Emotional responses often include shock, terror, depression, guilt, horror, irritability, hostility, and anxiety.
- Cognitive responses often include significant impairments in concentration, confusion, self-blame, flashbacks, decreased self-efficacy, and fears of losing control or trauma reoccurrences.

- Biologically-based responses include sleep disturbances, nightmares, insomnia, an exaggerated startle response, and other psychosomatic symptoms.
- Behavioral responses often include avoidance, social withdrawal, substance abuse, and interpersonal stress, such as decreased intimacy and trust in others.

ADULTHOOD

Erikson's described eight stages of psychosocial development through which a healthy human should pass when developing from infancy to late adulthood. He identified and described the following three different stages of adulthood, which include:

- Early Adulthood (approximately age 20 - 40) is the phase when most young people move from home, complete their schooling, and begin working full-time. Major concerns during this time are developing a career, establishing an intimate partnership, marrying and rearing children, or forming other lifestyles.
- Middle Adulthood (approximately age 40 - 60) is the phase when many people's careers are at their peak and they attain leadership roles. They help their children begin their own independent lives and help their parents cope with aging. People become increasingly aware of their own mortality as well.
- Late Adulthood (approximately age 60 years – death) is the phase when people adjust to decreased physical health and strength, retirement, and often to their spouse's death. They reflect on the meaning and significance of their lives.

ADULTS AND ART THERAPY

An effective therapist should use a range of counseling skills to engage the patient's inner life. By establishing rapport, the patient develops a conscious feeling of sympathy, harmonious accord, and mutual responsiveness with the therapist, contributes to the patience confidence in the therapist and his or her willingness to work cooperatively in therapy. By developing trust, the patient becomes willing to place themselves in a position of risk, or one such that the therapist's words, promises, or statements are reliable. By the therapist employing empathy (the willingness to take the patient's point of view) to understand the patient's experience without the therapist losing him or herself in that viewpoint, the therapist further builds trust and rapport.

THE ROLE OF MOTIVATION IN THE THERAPEUTIC PROCESS INVOLVING ADULTS

Motivation is an important initiating component toward any behavioral change or action. Many adults come to therapy voluntarily, which is an intrinsic motivation to overcome problems and relieve symptoms (anxiety, depression, embarrassment, etc.) and address deeper underlying problems. External motivation comes from outside the person. To understand the patient's motivation, the therapist needs to know what the patient's self-concept. The therapist's role is to help the patient change his or her self-perceptions and behavior by understanding the patient and foster a non-threatening atmosphere. Strategies and programs used to address the motivational needs of the patient include motivational enhancement therapy (MET), brief intervention, and motivational interviewing.

THE EFFECT OF RESISTANCE ON THE THERAPEUTIC PROCESS OF ADULTS

Resistance concerns to the patient's efforts (usually unconscious) to block treatment progress. Resistance occurs because the patient experiences fear or anxiety from uncovering unconscious material. It can take on many different forms, including delaying receiving of help, arriving late to sessions or forgetting to pay, and displaying hostility toward the therapist such as interrupting, ignoring, denying, arguing, and focusing on unimportant issues.

The therapist should be aware that a resistant client is providing important information about the patient's self-concept. Some causes commonly associate with resistance include the following:

- Lack of rapport between the patient and therapist
- Environmental factors or unhealthy dependency relationships or other external factors
- Patient factors like a hidden agenda, religion, culture, or lack of motivation

ROLE OF CULTURE

It is not possible to fully understood people by just examining their internal processes and identity. Instead, the therapeutic process should include the role of culture. To best develop an accurate picture of a patient's experiences and problems, the therapist must expand their understanding of the patient's situation to include social and cultural factors. One's background impacts normal verbal and nonverbal behaviors. Eye contact and appropriate physical proximity have different meanings and regularities in different cultures, as does formality of speech. In addition to awareness of the cultural impact of different behaviors, it can be helpful for thee therapist to adapt their own verbal and nonverbal behavior to the patient's culturally-based expectations. If a patient comes from a culture where direct eye contact is considered disrespectful for example, it is important for the therapist to adjust his or her own eye contact practices.

RELIGION AND SPIRITUALITY

Spirituality and religion influence a patient's world view, their cultural and societal interactions, and the ways in which they address their personal problems. The therapist must recognize the role that spirituality and religion play in normal human development and the process of making decisions. This information should be included in the regular therapy intake procedure as understanding this will facilitate sensitivity to the patient's beliefs and help the therapist better understand the patient as a whole person. The therapist should also be acknowledged and be aware of his or her own spiritual/religious beliefs, and to make these clear to the patient without imposing them on the patient.

CHILDHOOD TRAUMA ASSESSMENT TOOLS

Research clearly indicates that childhood trauma is a major cause of maladaptive functioning in adulthood. The aftermath of trauma in childhood can manifest at any age in a host of ways. Internally, it can appear as anxiety, PTSD, or suicidal thoughts. Outwardly, it can also be expressed as aggression, hyperactivity, impulsiveness, delinquency, or substance abuse.

Several assessment tools are available including:

- Comprehensive clinical interviews
- Structured interviews such as the Anxiety Disorders Interview Schedule-IV and the Clinician Administered PTSD scale
- Paper-and-pencil assessments
- The PTSD subscale from the Minnesota Multiphasic Personality Inventory (MMPI and MMPI-2), the Trauma Symptom Inventory, and the Penn Inventory for PTSD
- Useful screening instruments for anxiety and depression include the Beck Anxiety Inventory and the Second Edition Beck Depression Inventory
- The Stroop Color Word Test is a performance-based measure successfully used with patients who have experienced combat, rape, and disasters

ELDERLY

Most elderly adults prefer independent living. The United States government has recently started shifting elder care funding to encourage independent living. Oftentimes, the independent elder with age-related disabilities requires support services, such as low-income senior governmental housing, and private retirement villages/communities. Many factors affect a senior adult's independent living that are not related to the aging process itself, including:

- Grandparents raising grandchildren in the same home
- Increased life expectancy of those Developmentally-disabled family members cared for at home by their parents
- Children caring for and living with elderly family members
- Increasing percentage of single older adults who lack familial caregivers or support
- Emerging subgroups (like older AIDS patients) needing housing with specialized care or public policy attention (like appropriate housing for senior prisoners)

For elderly adults that cannot live independently, long-term care is available. Institutional care is primarily provided in nursing homes and facilities, which offer skilled nursing care for those recovering from acute illness episodes or chronic custodial care for those who are functionally impaired. There is an ongoing positive shift of housing settings rather than institutions providing health and long-term care with a range of supportive assistance. In the public and private sectors alike, economics drives this shift. However, this does not eliminate institutionalized care because sometimes, it is more cost-effective and appropriate to have elderly in a nursing facility instead of a home.

Assisted living or adult care homes provide a 24- hour care community integrating housing with a variety of supportive assistance, health services, and long-term care. Assisted living currently is the most popular institutional choice of older adults.

PROCESS OF AGING

In older adults, the cell regeneration rate and biological function rates decrease. Some of the biological aging changes include:

- Skin and Appearance -- Loss of skin elasticity and moisture, which results in wrinkles and skin that is thin and sags
- Hair -- Thins and grays or loses sheen
- Bones -- Loss of bone mass and elasticity, which leads to brittleness, osteoporosis, and a bowed back from spinal disc compression
- Senses and Reactions -- become slower and fuller so movements should be more cautious
- Reduction in acute senses like thirst and hunger
- Slowed responses
- Reduction in balance ability
- Memory and Learning
  - Learning ability does not usually decline, especially in those who routinely exercise their minds
  - Long-term memory typically remains sharp, even while short-term memory declines

ADAPTATIONS FOR THE ELDERLY WITH DISABILITIES

When elderly adults suffer from a disability that either impacts their physical or psychological abilities, their art therapist can adapt art media to accommodate their special needs so that they can still create personally meaningful and expressive artwork.

EXAMPLES OF MEDIA FORMS THAT MAY BE USED WITH VARIOUS DISABILITIES INCLUDE:

- Deficits in physical dexterity, such as shaking and lacking gross or fine motor control
  - Media that necessitates less control or that can assist with one's control like paint and clay
  - Sponge-covered paintbrush handle
  - Taping paper directly to the table
- Visual defects or deficits
  - Placing objects in the patient's visual field
  - Dark marker on light-colored paper
  - Separate paintbrushes in different tempera paint jars
  - Precut collage pictures

- Confused/suicidal patients
  - o Safe media (scissors and other sharp items that are modified)
  - o Nontoxic materials

DEVELOPMENTAL TASKS OF THE ELDERLY

Erikson felt that the mature adult's (age 65+) basic conflict is ego integrity versus despair and reflection on life is the most important event encountered during this period. Robert J. Havighurst in his Developmental Tasks and Education identifies the following six developmental tasks of later maturity:

- Adjusting to declining physical health and strength
- Adjusting to retirement
- Adjusting to death of one's partner
- Establishing an affiliation with one's age group and peers
- Adopting and adapting flexible social roles
- Establishing physical living arrangements that are satisfactory
- Developing a psychohistorical perspective

DEVELOPMENTALLY DISABLED

The law defines developmentally disabled a "severe and chronic disability" attributable to a physical or mental impairment or both that manifested before age 22 and which results in significant functional limitations in at least three major daily life activities, such as self-care, economic self-sufficiency, receptive and expressive language, mobility, learning, self-direction, and capacity for independent living. Usually individuals with intellectual disabilities, Fragile X syndrome or Down syndrome or other genetic and chromosomal disorders, cerebral palsy, autism spectrum disorder, and Fetal Alcohol disorder are considered as having developmental disabilities.

LOWENFELD AND HENLEY

Lowenfeld's approach to education is one of personal discovery and it emphasizes the importance of each individual child. Lowenfeld taught therapists to consider the child as a whole and examine his or her creative and mental development and artistic skills. He emphasized the various ways that art can improve self-esteem and offer and outlet of self-expression for children.

David Henley developed an art therapeutic approach for use with individuals with disabilities by using Viktor Lowenfeld's and Edith Kramer's ideas. He wrote *Exceptional Children: Exceptional Art* (1992, Davis Publications), a text that is considered a foundation or standard in the field, as well as *Clayworks in Art Therapy*. Dr. Henley is renowned for clinical experience in schools and hospital settings, where he worked with a wide range of deaf children or those with attention and social deficits. His unique research into animal art, working with dolphins, chimpanzees, and elephants in art therapeutic settings earned him notoriety.

COMMUNICATION ADAPTATIONS

Many developmentally disabled patients struggle with communication and pacing of speech, due to hearing loss, intellectual disability, neurological disorders, brain injury, physical impairments like cleft lip or palate, developmental disorders, or emotional or psychiatric disorders.

The most common communication modalities at the receiving end are sight and sound, and at the expressive end, voice and gesture. Helen Keller communicated on the receiving end through a tactile modality, Braille. Cross-channel communication is another viable means, whereby auditory stimuli occurs in the receptive process and the expressive response is motor in nature. Art therapists can address communication by using techniques such as multi-sensory methods that integrate the senses, shared drawing tasks, and mirroring, which is mimicking the patient's behavior and art expressions.

- The Face Stimulus Assessment (FSA) was developed for use with nonverbal patients or those with other communication disorders
- The Levick Emotional and Cognitive Art Therapy Assessment (LECATA) was developed for nonverbal exceptional children

FUNCTIONAL LEVEL AND IQ

An intelligence quotient (IQ) score is obtained from a set of standardized tests developed for measuring one's intelligence (cognitive abilities) relative to their age. Intelligence refers to abilities such as perceiving relationships or connections between ideas, completing an arithmetic series, and properly defining vocabulary terms.

The following is Wechsleher's 1997 (WAIS-III) Classification of the functional levels of IQ:

$$130 \text{ and over} = \text{Very superior}$$
$$120 - 129 = \text{Superior}$$
$$110 - 119 = \text{High average}$$
$$90 - 109 = \text{Normal or average intelligence}$$
$$80 - 89 = \text{Low average}$$
$$70 - 79 = \text{Borderline}$$
$$69 \text{ and under} = \text{Extremely low}$$

Similar groupings are seen in other classification systems.

ADAPTATIONS FOR ART

Art materials and techniques may need to be adapted according to the functional level of the intellectually-disabled patient.

The DSM has four different degrees or classifications of intellectual disability, which are based on the individual's functioning level.

- Mild: IQ score between 50–70. Often, these individuals can acquire academic skills up to approximately the sixth-grade level. They can also become fairly self-sufficient and potentially live independently, with adequate community and social support.
- Moderate: IQ score between 35–50. With moderate supervision, these individuals can perform work and self-care tasks. They can successfully live and function in the community in group homes or other supervised environments.
- Severe: IQ score between 20–35. These individuals may master very basic self-care and communication skills. Many can successfully live in a group home.
- Profound: IQ score less than 20. With appropriate support and training, they may be able to attain very basic self-care and communication skills. They require a lot of structure and supervision.

PHYSICALLY DISABLED

People may have many a wide variety of physical disabilities. An individual is considered physically disabled if they have a chronic physical handicap or impairment, whether from bodily injury, illness, or congenital, or from organic processes or changes over time. Included in this definition are conditions such as epilepsy, impaired hearing or deafness, reliance on a wheelchair or other assistive device, among many other conditions so long as it substantially limits one or more basic physical activities (i.e., walking, climbing stairs, carrying, reaching, or lifting).

ADAPTING ART MATERIALS AND TECHNIQUES FOR CLIENTS WITH SPECIFIC DISABILITIES

As more people with physical disabilities engage in art making, more adaptive devices and technologies are being developed to better facilitate their expression and participation.

- Artists lacking use of their hands can use a mouth-stick or supported paint brush, which allow the artist to work for long periods of time comfortably.
- Artists with limited strength and mobility can be facilitated with motorized easels or adjustable-height drafting boards, both which can be angled and` positioned by flipping a switch or pushing a button.
- An artist's field of vision can be improved with magnification devices.
- Individuals with motor coordination issues that cause difficulties in painting, cutting, gluing, and may benefit from precut materials.
- There are video cameras, computers for those with quadriplegia, and assistive devices for bedridden individuals.
- Wheelchair art involves rolling the chair through colored paint pools and then through items or onto surfaces.

SECONDARY FACTORS RELATED TO PHYSICAL TRAUMA

Physical trauma is a serious shock or injury to the body from causes such as violence, surgery, or an accident. Oftentimes, the rehabilitation process is accompanied with significant physical and mental pain. The patient who has experienced a serious or life-threatening physical injury can potentially develop secondary emotional issues such as depression, specific phobias, generalized anxiety, agoraphobia, dissociation and psychosis, suicidal thoughts, depersonalization, derealization, self-mutilation, auditory hallucinations, panic attacks, eating disorders, hypervigilance, social phobia, recurring nightmares, social abuse, and flashbacks.

SPECIALIZED MATERIALS AND TOOLS FOR CLIENTS WITH EMOTIONAL STRESS DUE TO PHYSICAL TRAUMA

Little qualitative/quantitative research regarding art therapy and trauma currently exists. Most of the conducted research has come from other professions that also specialize in psychological trauma. The Silver Drawing Test of Cognition and Emotion (SDT), Draw a Story (DAS), and Stimulus Drawings and Techniques (SDS) employ stimulus and response drawings access feelings, fantasies, and thoughts that may be verbally inaccessible. These assessments are also used as pre-post tests to measure changes in emotional status and cognitive ability. Oftentimes, group therapy is helpful because it gives patients with similar physical disability the ability to share thoughts and feelings with one another. Some patients may have physical conditions that make it quite difficult to make art, but with adaptations and well-designed assistive devices, it is usually workable.

WITHDRAWAL

Withdrawal encompasses the characteristic resultant signs and symptoms when a physically-dependent drug that has been regularly used for quite some time is suddenly discontinued or tapered significantly.

The symptoms of withdrawal include:

- Alcohol withdrawal -- simple shakes, DT, disorientation, altered mental status, seizures, hallucinations
- Opioid withdrawal -- Can resemble severe flu, with symptoms like rhinorrhea, sneezing, lacrimation, abdominal cramping, yawning, leg cramping, piloerection, nausea, vomiting, dilated pupils, and diarrhea.
- Stimulants -- Dysphoria, hunger, excessive sleep, and significant, psychomotor retardation
- GHB -- Relatively mild withdrawal resembles sedative-hypnotic withdrawal syndrome, which is characterized by brief and mild autonomic instability with prolonged psychotic symptoms.

- GHB -- Significant withdrawal, with symptoms like those of alcohol-withdrawal syndrome, except that delirium occurs early and there are no seizures.
- Sedative-hypnotic withdrawal -- significant psychomotor and autonomic dysfunctions.

DUAL DIAGNOSIS

Dual diagnosis is a commonly used, broad term that refers to the simultaneous presence of two separate medical disorders, such as an individual diagnosed with a major mental disorder and an addiction. In this case. The addiction can mask and/or exacerbate other psychological symptoms and the person may use drugs and alcohol as "medication" to handle the psychological symptoms. Patients with dual diagnoses have a decreased treatment response if one of their disorders goes untreated. To fully recover, the individual needs treatment for both problems.

In more recent years, recognition that many patients with severe mental illness are unwilling or unable to engage in traditional community-based services, the emphasis in the mental health field has been on case management. Case management can be an effective way of reducing the negative consequences to the patient from their lack of treatment participation and follow-up.

SUPPORT GROUPS

Support groups permit individuals with a common diagnosis to meet together, share coping tips and experiences, and provide critical emotional support. The 12-step program provides a set of guiding principles for addiction recovery, or those recovering from compulsive or behavioral problems. The program was originally developed by Alcoholics Anonymous (A.A.) fellowship to guide alcoholism recovery, but has since been adapted to form the foundation of other rehab programs such as Overeaters Anonymous, Codependents Anonymous, Narcotics Anonymous, and Crystal Meth Anonymous. Mandated court involvement with various 12-Step programs is a controversial practice employed by some governments.

Basic concepts of these programs involve:

- Admitting one's serious, uncontrollable problem
- Acknowledging that outside power may help
- Conscious and continued reliance upon that identified power
- Identifying and admitting one's character deficits
- Seeking deliverance from these deficits
- Making amends to those individuals one has harmed
- Helping and supporting others facing the same problem

SAFETY ISSUES
CHEMICALLY-DEPENDENT

Certain art products can be harmful to the patient if inhaled, ingested, or absorbed through the skin. Only those products that carry the ACMI AP seal (that identifies medical expert certified toxicological evaluation art products that contain no materials in toxic or dangerous quantities to humans) should be used. The labels HL (Health Label) and CP (Certified Product) are also non-toxic and certified by ACMI as labeled with ASTM D 4236 (the chronic hazard labeling standard). A trained therapist knows not to offer an unstable or labile patients certain materials like sharp, pointed tools.

THE PHYSICALLY ILL

Illnesses can be either acute and chronic. Acute illnesses are generally over fairly quickly, while chronic illnesses are usually long-lasting. Although chronic illness symptoms may go away with medical care, the patient still has the underlying condition. When properly treated, the patient may feel totally healthy most of the time. It should be noted that chronic illness can only be managed, but not cured. Some conditions are relatively mild, while others cause significant functional impairments and may shorten one's lifespan.

Basic healthcare safety for those with acute or chronic medical illness includes:

- Knowledge and awareness of common symptoms
- Utilizing basic practices of sound hygiene, including covering the nose and mouth when coughing or sneezing, hand washing, and maintaining a clean work environment
- Keeping immunizations up-to-date

GRIEF

The intent of grief work is not to help the patient "get over" loss, but rather to help them adjust to its consequences and restore workable balance. The grief work stages include:

- Facing the loss and its ramification
- Working through painful memories and feelings
- Experiencing the entire range of emotions associated with the loss
- Coping with or adapting to the situational and lifestyle changes caused by the loss
- Reconfiguring one's own life to accommodate the loss

The creative art making experience employed during the time of traumatic loss affords the opportunity for growth, self-exploration, and healing. Art therapy can support the patient's need to creatively express grief and it can help prevent behavioral, psychological, and social problems that result from unresolved grief. In addition, empathy and connection are fortified by the process of making art together in a group.

BEREAVEMENT

Bereavement refers to the period after a loss when grief and mourning are experienced. The terms grief and bereavement are often incorrectly used interchangeably. Bereavement is more than just grief and loss; it encompasses many issues and deals with coping and adapting through a hard time in one's life. It is typically accompanied by significant stress in everyday life. Following a significant loss, reactions can include shock and numbness, disorganization and despair, feeling of separation, and reorganization. There is no defined standard for what is considered healthy and unhealthy in bereavement, yet there are warning signs of poor adjustment including:

- Coping by avoiding
- Feeling loneliness and desolated like there is no reason to go on without the loved one anymore
- Detachment from all people around them (surviving siblings and family, friends)
- Overbearing attachment to other people

REALITY TESTING

Reality testing, a widely used term in clinical psychology, refers to an individual's ability to objectively differentiate between their inner imaginative world and the external world. Psychotic disorders occur when reality testing yields a significant disturbance, which may be manifested by delusions, hallucinations, or thinking disturbances. Reality testing disturbances are associated with conditions such as bipolar disorder, schizophrenia, and psychotic depression, which are conditions with a high degree of morbidity, disability, and sometimes, mortality.

DENIAL AND MANIPULATION

By avoiding or denying personal responsibility for their actions, patients with acute or chronic psychiatric illness often exhibit their dependency needs by manipulating or lying to the people around them in their desperate attempt for others to take care of them. They transfer responsibility and blame to others and often develop delusions about the external world such that they can create a sense of responsibility in others for their own personal good and welfare. Such a sense of responsibility can extend to paying bail money, credit card debt, lawyer fees, etc. Families often accommodate these behaviors by slowing the treatment progress.

ARNHEIM, PRINZHORN, AND ARIETI

The works of Rudolf Arnheim, Hans Prinzhorn, and Silvano Arieti are instrumental in understanding the ways in which psychiatric illness manifests itself in artwork.

- Rudolf Arnheim is a pioneering art psychology theorist. In *Art as Visual Perception* (one of several of his influential works), he refers to human consciousness on all levels (from dreams to hallucinations) as "Visual Thinking."
- Hans Prinzhorn wrote The Artistry of the Mentally Ill, a work that contains an analysis of artwork created by the mentally disabled. His collection has remained most valuable source of art created by mentally disabled patients and it continues to be a reference for many scholars in the field.

- Silvano Arieti, an Italian psychiatrist, focused on the link between schizophrenic disorders and creativity. He edited the reference guide American Handbook of Psychiatry. Arieti coined the phrase "tertiary process" as a way of explaining his belief that creativity is a unique thought form.

STRESS AND THE INSTITUTIONALIZED

Some patients, at an immediate risk of relapse, need continued inpatient treatment to address ongoing medical or psychiatric issues or illnesses. When an individual has been institutionalized in a hospital, nursing home, or prison, either voluntarily or involuntarily, stress from quality of life declines and or low self-esteem can play an important role in the patient's recovery. Stress management interventions are necessary and should begin with a review of diagnostic findings, current care program, rehabilitation plans, and realistic encouragement and training to achieve rehabilitation goals successfully. This should occur with the patient and his or her family, friends, or support.

VOLUNTARY VS. INVOLUNTARY COMMITMENT

Institutional commitments can be of the following types:

- Voluntary commitment: individual freely chooses to be admitted to a psychiatric facility or hospital
- Involuntary commitment: filed petition aims to commit a person who is judged dangerous to themselves or others

Each state imposes laws to regulate care and treatment of those with mentally illness. Such laws aim to balance the protection of the mentally ill patient's civil rights with public safety preservation. Because an individual may be unwillingly committed to an institution, strict legal procedures exist to protect their civil rights. State laws also allow individuals to apply for voluntary admission or commitment for treatment to any facility. This procedure involves an individual presenting to a facility and participating in an examination by trained admission personnel, who determine if the individual would indeed benefit from treatment.

LENGTH-OF-STAY

There are no standard psychiatric inpatient length-of-stay guidelines as there are for certain medical conditions. Instead, the length of inpatient treatment for psychiatric conditions is subject to significant variation.

Ideally, psychiatric patients are discharged when they no longer pose a danger to themselves or others and the goals of treatment have been achieved. Involuntarily committed patients cannot leave whenever they want; instead, discharges always require a doctor's written approval. A patient's length of stay is usually specified in emergency commitments. A voluntarily admitted person must be released immediately upon submission of a written request. If such a patient requests discharge without a doctor's order, the patient signs a statement that the discharge is taking place against medical advice (AMA). Without following discharge procedures, voluntarily committed patient may leave the facility.

ART THERAPIST ON TEAM

Art therapy is frequently one part of a psychiatric outpatient it inpatient treatment program, and it can take place in either individual or group therapy settings. Art therapists work with patients of all ages in rehabilitative, clinical, educational, and medical settings in adjunctive capacities. Art therapists may evaluate patients, set treatment objectives and goals, develop treatment plans, provide case management services, and deliver therapeutic treatment. Oftentimes, group art therapy sessions take place in hospitals, community programs, clinics, and shelters.

Interdisciplinary health teams have grown in long-term care, reflecting the emphasis on the biopsychosocial model of clinical work for use with residents. Information gained primarily through nonverbal processes is usually helpful to all treatment team members to attain a more complete and well-rounded view of the patient.

Common job duties include the following:

- Conferring with other allied health professionals regarding the objectives and goals for each patient
- Assessing patient needs to best prescribe a personalized creative arts treatment plan or program
- Using observations and interviews to evaluate patients' responses to creative art therapies
- Developing and implementing creative arts activities, such as singing, playing drums, dancing, and making clay objects
- Working with patients individually and using the arts as a means of encouraging self-expression
- Teaching patients necessary basic skills to engage in creative arts, such as a dance step, how to use pottery wheels, mime
- Maintaining records on patient progress and helping with discharge planning

DAY TREATMENT PROGRAMS

A day treatment program is an active, time-limited treatment program with structured daily classes, coordinated and structured clinical services, and individual and group therapy sessions that patients attend during the day and then go home in the evening. Included clinical services are psychology, communication, medicine, psychiatry, nursing, social work, and recreation. The treatment team often includes a board-certified psychiatrist, psychiatric nurses, licensed therapists, activities/recreational therapists, mental health technicians, and educational coordinators who combine their skills together to offer an intensive, daily, therapeutic experience. These programs also provide family members with education and support.

DISCHARGE PLANNING

Day treatment program discharge planning focuses on support outside the program. State and federal law guarantee the patient's right to participate in the aftercare or discharge plan development. A discharge plan is developed with the patient and/or caretaker, psychiatrists, psychologists, social workers, housing professionals, and other community partners to create the patient's discharge plan.

The following elements are part of discharge plan:

- Nature of illness and required follow-up
- Medications, side effects, and prescribed dosage schedules. Of note, if the patient was provided with an informed consent form with the medication, the form satisfies the requisite information on the medication side effects)
- Expected recovery course
- Treatment recommendations relevant to the patient's care and condition
- Referrals to medical and mental health providers
- Other relevant information as needed

IMPACT OF THE SETTING

Security issues must be prioritized over therapeutic interventions in a correctional facility. Personal boundaries must be maintained to ensure the physical safety of both patients and staff. The art therapist needs to achieve a careful balance of reinforcing security standards and structure while simultaneously encouraging individual artistic expression and productivity. Incorporating artwork into the therapeutic relationship helps empower patients to expressive themselves in an environment that otherwise demands obedience and passivity without risking the facility's safety. In nursing homes, residents may have concurrent medical and psychological disorders, which can result in high rates of dementia, depression, and other mental disorders. Patients may be nonsocial, nonverbal, blind, and/or immobile. Art can be a tool that reconnects them with a healthier time in their lives.

OLMSTEAD VS. L.C.

When an individual can no longer care for themselves, they receive long-term care, which includes a variety of mostly non-medical services designed to help recipients maintain as much independence as possible. An institution includes a set of buildings and associated grounds that provide essential services to residents, such as housing, food, education, and treatment on a 24-hour-a-day full-time basis.

In the landmark Supreme Court ruling, Olmstead vs. L.C., the court decided via the Americans with Disabilities Act that states must administer their activities, services, and programs "in the most integrated setting appropriate to the needs of qualified individuals with disabilities."

OPEN STUDIOS APPROACH

A recent art therapy movement makes use of open studios and groups as a way to provide art access to individuals in wheelchairs and mobility braces and intercity clients. The clinical setting is removed when open studios are used for art therapy. These spaces may be a community place that encourages creativity in participants of any age and background. Like in a psychiatric institutional setting, in an open studio setting, a patient can voluntarily come and use art materials. In a community based program, the patient can work independently or in a group and art materials are provided.

CULTURAL BACKGROUND

Culture is multifaceted and helps individuals find meaning and form relationships. Therapists may encounter cultural differences including the following:

- Some cultures feel that the "disability" is spiritual or a reward or blessing for ancestral tribulations rather than physical.
- Some patients' ideas about the body's structure and function may differ from those of the therapist
- Some patients may believe they have a "folk illness", which is an illness undefined by traditional biomedicine
- Body language and terminology may be understood or interpreted differently (for example, in Anglo-American culture, a firm handshake symbolizes strong character, yet in some Native American cultures, a limp handshake symbolizes respect and humility.)

Different cultures maintain different concepts of community, self, and family that impact interventions as they influence interpersonal relationships and social interactions. Some examples of these differing concepts include:

- Westerners tend to separate personal and professional identity while many cultures value both roles in personal relationships.
- Family includes extended family members outside of the traditional nuclear family for some patients and these relatives may be involved in the decision-making process for various treatment decisions
- Many patients who identify with racial and ethnic minority groups prefer to work with mental health professionals from similar backgrounds.
- Some patients avoid direct eye contact because of cultural or personal preferences

Therapists who work with a diverse population need to recognize and respond to hurdles in therapy posed by these types of differences (for example, "You're different than me, so how can you understand this?"). There is currently an insufficient number of mental health professionals from racial and ethnic minority populations.

With a fundamental respect for patients and appropriate training, any mental health professional can offer culturally competent services that are sensitive to individual differences and simultaneously validate an individual's group identity. Services that are "Culturally competent" include:

- Foster a welcoming and attractive environment based on clients' cultural ideals
- Avoid stereotyping and inaccurately applying scientific knowledge
- Incorporate continuous community input during the planning and development stages
- Employ educational materials and approaches that will capture the intended audience's attention
- Recognize that there is no single "correct" solution to every problem
- Hire staff that reflects the patient population
- Recognize that cultural competency is always evolving
- Find communicate methods for population groups with limited English-speaking proficiency or comfort

A common mistake in working with individuals from is to stereotype them. Stereotypes, by definition, are standardized common mental pictures held by members of a group representative of critical judgement, oversimplified opinions, and prejudiced attitudes. Stereotypes influence an individual's perception process and his or her judgement and behavior. In considering cultural issues, there is a tendency toward stereotyping.

The therapist should become aware of the patient's culture and continuously challenge any personal or widespread existing biases that may create barriers to providing effective professional services. "Catch-terms" often lump people together regardless of the real sub-cultural variations that actually exists within minority populations. It is critically important for therapists to avoid passing something off as determined or caused by a person's cultural beliefs, when in reality, it is determined or caused by social factors like poverty and/or single parent homes that contribute to a non-adaptive or restricted social life.

Racial, gender, and ethnic differences can bring various perceptions of psychotherapy that affect the relationship between patients and therapists. Limited research has indicated that members of ethnic and racial minority groups frequently perceive that the existing system's offered services cannot or will not meet their needs based on their cultural, linguistic, or religious practices.

Certain personality disorders (Borderline, Histrionic), according to the DSM, are more common among women, while rates of others (Paranoid, Narcissistic, Antisocial, Schizotypal, Schizoid, and Obsessive-Compulsive) are higher in men.

Barriers that often prevent racial and ethnic minority patients from seeking mental health services include:

- Treatment mistrust and fear
- Different cultural ideas about health and illnesses
- Differences in help-seeking behaviors, communication patterns, and language
- Racism
- Varying insured vs. uninsured rates
- Individual and institution-based discrimination

Additionally, all populations with mental disorders are negatively affected by fragmented or unavailable services, high costs, and societal stigma.

CULTURAL FACTORS THAT INFLUENCE AN INDIVIDUAL'S ATTITUDE TOWARD ART

Minorities' historical and current struggles with discrimination and racism contribute to their lower political, economic, and social status and affect their attitude and access toward mental health services. Elements of culture (such as religious authority figures, rites, and rituals) may influence thinking, feeling, and behavior that, in turn, determine the way in which a patient produces art. Additional factors include the patient's individual life circumstances, such as their age, gender, spiritual beliefs, and sexual orientation. An individual's culture affects the way in which color is used and the creation of specific artifacts like totem poles and masks. Most therapists lack skills for understanding these various cultural influences and the way to best help craft culturally appropriate interventions.

Art Theory and Media

ART MUSEUMS

An art museum, either one with a single exhibit or one with many, is another viable environment for learning outside of more traditional clinical settings. An art museum visit provides opportunities for the patient to learn different practices from different people. Opportunities for patients include:

- The chance to explore the reasons the artwork was created
- To reflect on what the artist has selected to leave out of the depicted image
- To consider the reasons that the artist has included each component in the image.
- To determine the story the image conveys
- To compare how different works are the same and different from one another
- Self-expression can be fostered by tasking the patient to:
- Add a line or component to the story
- Select an artwork and draw what he or she sees in the image

VARIETY OF SOURCES

Art therapy is founded on the assumption that visual images and symbols are the most natural and accessible form of communication from human self-expression. Patients are encouraged to visualize and use artwork to express the thoughts and emotions otherwise too difficult or painful to verbally share. Then, the patient reviews the resulting artwork and interprets its meaning. Humans can learn from a wide variety of sources. Visual aids such as slides, films, posters, and books can be used to stimulate a patient's expression and creativity. For example, when patients cannot use their hands or are uncomfortable using the art materials, photographic images or postcards can be reviewed and discussed.

ROLE OF DESIGN ELEMENTS

The various elements of design can be used to allow patients to express difficult feelings and attain a better self-concept. Line, form, color, shape, space, and can be used when creating a work of art as follows:

- Lines typically imply motion and suggest direction, which can convey mood.
- Form refers to the three-dimensional arrangement of lines into figures like pyramids, spheres, cones, cylinders, and cubes, and cylinders.
- Geometric shapes, compared to natural ones, are more passive, decorative, and static. Movement can be created with repeated shapes.
- Space and size can be used to denote significance by making certain things appear nearer than others and of greater importance. Depth can be created by playing with size relationships. Positive space is formed by objects that are viewed as a main element appearing to be positioned in front of the background.

105

- Colors can have a warm or cool quality. Warm colors are highly visible and appear to come toward the viewer. Cool colors seem to recede from the viewer.
- Compositional movement is the manner of the viewer's eye movement through a given composition. Static movement jumps between a composition's isolated parts. Dynamic movement flows smoothly between various parts of the composition.

SYMBOLISM

A symbol is often used to convey something inexpressible. An object may be symbolic to an artist and understanding the symbol's personal significance to the patient helps to appreciate the patient's work. For example, the American flag, to an American citizen, can symbolize patriotism. The dove is a fairly universal symbol of peace. The cross symbolizes Christianity, and the star with six points symbolizes Judaism in many regions. The symbolism of different colors varies from culture to culture. In American culture, black is often associated with death or sophistication and formality, while white signifies life and purity. However, in some Asian cultures, white is the traditionally the color of mourning. Americans often associate blue with trust and stability, while pink and other pastel colors symbolizes these feelings in the Korean culture.

HISTORY OF SYMBOLISM

Symbolism, as a term, refers to the systematic use of pictorial conventions or symbols to express an allegorical meaning. Originating in France and Belgium in late nineteenth century, symbolism was impacted by Freud's psychoanalytical work. Symbolism art introduced dream imagery and mythology mysticism into visual art. Symbolism's symbols are intensely personal, ambiguous, private, and obscure references rather than familiar emblems of mainstream iconography. Symbolism is an important aspect of most religious arts and understanding symbols plays is a critical role in psychoanalytic practice.

SYMBOLS ARE COLLECTIVE CREATIONS

A symbol is often a product of group experiences and helps shape a group's future needs and experiences. An individual's sense of group identity can be influenced by adhering to the group's common attachment to a shared symbol.

An American society, a few commonly shared symbols include:

- Common rituals: Graduations, weddings, club initiations, and baptisms
- Holidays: Christmas, Easter, Ramadan, Spring Break, Independence Day
- People: Celebrities, heroes and heroines, rebels
- Religious symbols: Star of David, Christian fish symbol, Yin and Yang, cross
- Colors: Red – danger; Pink – feminine; Blue – masculine
- Numbers: 13 – Unlucky; 3 - Trinity indicating the Father, Son, & Holy Spirit;
- Animals: Dove – Peace; Eagle - the Great Spirit to American Indians; Owl – Wisdom

- Gestures: Thumb(s) up for approval; "V" for victory, peace
- Political: Elephant; Donkey

COMIC BOOKS

The media of comic books began in the 1930s with comic strips and cartoons compiled together in a manner designed to appeal to young adult males. The subject matter of comic books is frequently dramatic, serious, violent, and sexual, with themes often addressing dreams and archetypal situations (such as the battle for deliverance or the hero's quest). Comic book superheroes were usually modeled after the main characters in popular American fiction of the time, often resembling a middle- to upper- class, white, heterosexual male professional, between the ages of 20 and 30. Today, most superheroes still fit this description; yet, beginning in the 1960s to attract a broader audience, many characters featured were anti-heroes, female, or non-Caucasians. In the 1960s, comic books started to be recognized as a serious art medium among art museums, academics, and literary critics with established traditions, artistic evolution, and stylistic conventions.

COLORS, NUMBERS, SYMBOLS, IMAGES

Not all images, colors, numbers, and symbols translate well across countries and cultures. Art therapists should understand and effectively apply this knowledge to their art therapy practice. Some cultures have lucky colors, such as red in Chinese culture, while others have unlucky colors, like black in Japanese culture. Some colors carry certain significance; green is a special color in Islamic culture, and some colors carry tribal associations in parts of Africa. Certain numbers have negative connotations. For example, many USA or UK hotels do not have a 13th floor. Japanese Nippon Airways omits seat numbers 4 and 9. In many European cities, it is common to see advertising photos of women in bikinis, but in the Middle East, such images might cause outrage. Native Americans are often offended when museums display images depicting sacred places and religious ceremonies. Important collective symbols, such as religious images like the cross, the Buddhist wheel of life, and the Star of David also exist.

TELEVISION

Television shows have long been a tool for interpreting the world. Advertising promotes "buying" as an American ideal. Conspicuously placement of a purchasable product on a television program is now both commonplace and profitable. Research has demonstrated that the use of symbols, words, and pictures often affect the viewing audience cognitively, emotionally, and behaviorally. Since the introduction of television, image-based persuasion in human lives has significantly increased. When used skillfully, these images can affect people's responses to the other information.

Pop art is a type of art based on popular images that are derived from both commercial and mass media sources permeating modern American society. Television shapes the way people view the world, and art reflects this experience. Robert Rauschenberg has incorporated images from popular culture in his paintings with techniques that imparts a grainy look and collaged image arrangement seen on television. Other artists have also incorporated the visual look and images from television into their artwork. Examples include Andy Warhol's soup cans, movie stars, and coke bottles.

TWO-DIMENSIONAL ART

A two-dimensional object has a height and width but lacks depth. An object's shape is classified as a two-dimensional element. Two-dimensional art media includes art work such as paintings, photographs, drawings, and prints that exist on a flat surface or page. Typical media include pen and ink, pencil, charcoal, pastels, acrylic paint, colored pencils, and watercolor. Two-dimensional compositions include design elements like line, value, shape, color, and texture. While true depth or distance are lacking in such works, artists create the illusion of distance or depth (or three-dimensions) on these flat surfaces using techniques such as overlapping, changing placement and size, linear or atmospheric perspective, and relative hue and value.

THREE-DIMENSIONAL MEDIA

Height, width, and depth gives volume or mass to three-dimensional objects such as cylinders, pyramids, spheres, cubes, and cones. Three-dimensional art items include sculpture, furniture, architecture, jewelry, and ceramics. Examples of three-dimensional media include marble, metal, bronze, clay, and paper maché. The space occupied by the form is called positive, while the empty space in and around the form is called negative space. Rectilinear shapes usually suggest stability while angular shapes positioned diagonally relative to gravity often suggest instability. Shapes with gently curving surfaces suggest sensuality, quiet, and comfort.

IMPACT OF VISUAL DATA

Vision accounts for approximately 60%–80% of the information processed by a person's brain. People learn and communicate through what they observe. Many psychologists have concerns about the negative impact of the typical subject matter communicated via visual media such as the Internet, television, and film, and their roles in shaping an individual's behavior. Such media is believed to promote racism, anti-social behavior, sex, and violence among some young people. Additionally, it is believed to impact the acquisition of reading skills and potential learning.

FACTORS DETERMINING APPROPRIATENESS

The following factors determine the appropriateness of different two- or three-dimensional media:

- What the patient is attracted to
- What the patient finds non-threatening
- What the art therapist is most knowledgeable about or experienced with
- The art therapist's assessment of the patient

- The therapeutic goals
- The patient's demographics

No matter if the art material is used in individual or group settings, the various media employed should be simple and unstructured, but also sturdy and of a good quality for durability. Usually, a wide selection of media should be provided. The media section will often be determined by the planned exercise. Specific examples include a family history genogram, three-dimensional materials for children with learning disabilities (they often respond best to artwork that is hands-on artwork), and for adults with neurological impairments, free-drawing, finger-painting, and mask-making.

PHYSICAL QUALITIES OF MEDIA

Art media possess characteristics such brightness, color, slope, lightness, uniformity, density, size, roughness, regularity, linearity, directionality, frequency, phase, coarseness, randomness, smoothness, fineness, and overall texture granulation.

Texture refers to the quality of the surface that light reveals. It is an important visual cue indicative of the properties of a surface. A material's surface quality is either considered actual (tactile) or implied (visual). The intensity of a color refers to its brightness or dullness.

Color can affect the artwork's mood and feeling conveyed.

A material's density refers to its ability to absorb light; the darker the material, the greater its density. The term also describes form and refers to the material's bulk, weight, and mass.

SUITABLE ART MATERIAL

Because the creative process is a primary goal in art therapy, the materials employed are often relatively simple and unstructured. Wherever possible, the following materials can be used for creative expression:

- Drawing materials include regular and colored pencils, felt pens, oil pastels or Craypas, felt pens, and crayons and markers. Drawing materials allow for finer control and detail.
- Paintings materials include watercolor, tempera paints, and special card stock. Painting, through color and brushstroke, encourages self-expression of feelings.
- Collage materials include pre-cut magazine or advertising images, construction and tissue paper, white or glitter glue, string, or yarn. Collage stimulates the imagination, provides structure, and is easy to control.
- Modeling materials include Model Magic, water-based clay, PlayDoh, and plasticine. Modeling with these materials offers the opportunity to create in three-dimensions and to reconstruct and rework.

MATERIAL PREPARATION AND STORAGE

The patient's age and disability is another determining factor in the patient's involvement in the art materials' preparation and storage. Some patients will be unfamiliar with art materials so the therapist show demonstrate what each material can do and how to safely use them. For example, patients should be taught basic brush-holding skills, how to mix paints, and how to properly apply paint to a surface. A structured and safe environment for creativity should be fostered and it should support the patient's freedom to use art self-expression. A safety checklist can be an effective way to control potential hazards and should be regularly used. Patients can act as "safety inspectors" to help with this responsibility.

The length of art therapy session varies depending on the guidelines and situational circumstances. In institutions, individual and group art therapy sessions may be time-limited, often from 50 minutes to a couple hours, or even shorter if working with children.

In a closed group wellness program, each session involves creating art, a group share and discussion of the art activity, and sometimes a second expressive modality, like journaling, which may last a few hours.

Managed care and liability have significantly affected the patient's and therapist's roles in the art therapy session. Exposure to toxic materials is best limited as much as possible, but if they are used, they should be in accordance with all labeled cautions and directions. Exposure to hazardous fumes and vapors is minimized when the art therapist premixes any dry materials with water and heats ceramic products when patients are not near the kiln. When working with children younger than grade seven or with adults unable to understand safety labels, art therapists should only use nontoxic art products.

It is inappropriate to expect young children to follow instructions regarding the proper use of arts and crafts products. Some art projects involve complicated or hazardous processes that inappropriate for small children, such as airbrushing, enameling, soldering, and photo developing. Art therapists should avoid projects involving these processes when working with young children.

SAFETY ISSUES

Understanding the proper use of various materials makes them safer for patients. It is important to be knowledgeable or able to judge the safety of various art materials for patients based on ability, allergies, age, and other relevant considerations. Art therapists should do the following:

- Consult lists of acceptable art and craft materials published for each state. Hazardous products require ASTM D-4236 on their labels, which is part of the U.S labeling law, ensuring proper testing has been conducted and the product is non-toxic and poses no health hazards.

- Only products with ACMI Non-Toxic Seals [CP, AP, and HL (Non-Toxic)] should be purchased and used with young children, patients with physical or mental disabilities, and those who cannot read or comprehend the safety labeling on material packages.
- The nonprofit Art and Creative Materials Institute (ACMI) is a trade association of art and craft product manufacturers. ACMI-AP indicates that the product is certified nontoxic. ACMI-CL ("Caution Label") denotes that the product contains toxic or hazardous ingredients, but with appropriate caution, it can be used safely.

SHARP TOOLS

Some of the tools used in an art therapy session are potentially dangerous. The following safety guidelines should be implemented:

- Tools with sharp points, like scissors or certain paint brushes, should be avoided.
- The selection of media provided should be void of the potential for destructive use. The therapist should explain that tools have a variety of functions but should only be used in safely and for creative purposes.
- Any item not being used in safely and for creative purpose should be removed.
- Therapists should be attentive for potential patients who may put materials such as paintbrushes in their mouth.

HANDLING TOXIC PRODUCTS

It is the responsibility of the art therapist to provide their patients with a safe environment for art sessions. The following guidelines help ensure proper handling and storage of toxic materials:

- Material containers should be unbreakable and clearly marked as to their contents, potential hazards, and date received and first opened.
- To prevent escape of vapors or dust, all original containers or the unbreakable ones that the material has been transferred to should be tightly closed except when the material is being used.
- A current inventory listing all materials on hand should be maintained, also detailing their locations and purchase date in order to dispose limited shelf-life materials appropriately.
- Materials should be stored amounts expected to be used within two months.
- Flammable or combustible materials should be purchased in small quantities because large quantities of such materials can pose a serious fire hazard.
- Locations of highly toxic or flammable materials should be posted.
- Cleaning supplies for handling spills should be kept on hand.
- Gloves, respiratory protection, and other personal protective equipment should be kept the studio at all times.

- An eye wash station and/or emergency shower should be available if chemical corrosives or chemicals are to be stored.
- Approved fire extinguishers or protection should be available.

Professionalism and Ethics

PROFESSIONAL DOCUMENTS

The following are some professional documents that offer content detailing the professional standards and ethics applicable to art therapy practice and what the art therapist should understand:

- ATCB Code of Professional Practice
  - A document that provides ethical practice guidelines.
- AATA Code of Ethics for Art Therapists
  - A document that formed the ATCB Code of Professional Practice's foundation, and that also provides important guidelines for art therapy ethical practice.
- AATA General Standards of Practice Document
  - A document that provides the general principles regarding psychotherapy professional and ethical practice that also apply to art therapy practice.

Additionally, each state's licensing laws define what the legally permissible art therapy services.

CLIENT RIGHTS

All therapy participants have certain rights that, during the course of therapy, must be maintained. These include one's right to an environment free of abuse, one's right to ask questions regarding therapy and receive an understandable answer, one's right to expect therapy to be helpful, and one's right to be treated respectfully as a unique individual. A patient has the right to expect the art therapist to do the following:

- Advance the patient's welfare
- Respect the patient's rights who seek services
- Use therapeutic services appropriately
- Respect and adequately protect confidential patient information obtained in conversation as well as via artistic expression.
- Refrain from any reproduction or public use of the patients' art from therapy sessions, including art expression and dialogue, without explicit patient written consent.
- Maintain high standards of professional integrity and competence.

PROVIDING ART THERAPY SERVICES

The American Art Therapy Association monitors art therapy in the United States and art therapists should be registered (ATR) as well as board-certified (ATR-BC). In some states, art therapists are also licensed by state licensing boards. To professionally enter the art therapy field, the art therapist needs to hold at least an

American Art Therapy Association (AATA) approved Master's degree. Graduates of AATA-approved degree programs must also accrue 1,000 direct patient contact hours before applying to the Art Therapy Credentials Board. Graduates hailing from non-approved degree programs must accrue at least 2,000 hours. In both cases, at least half of the required 100 hours of supervision must have been under a registered art therapist (ATR). Those art therapists registered with the Art Therapy Credentials Board are then eligible to take the national certification examination in art therapy. Those who pass the exam earn a "-BC" after the "ATR", resulting in Art Therapist, Registered, Board-Certified. A recertification program is also offered through the ATCB.

LIMITATIONS OF CONFIDENTIALITY

When a patient starts therapy, the art therapist needs to inform them of the confidentiality limitations regarding patient records and artwork. The following explain how the art therapist should disclose confidential information:

- With the patient or guardian's written consent and approval
- With reasonable belief that the patient or others are in severe, immediate danger to life or health
- In accordance with all laws pertaining to the patient, family, and general public's welfare.
- When it is in the patient's best interest
  - o Prior to any disclosures, whenever possible, the art therapist should seek the patient or guardian's written consent.
  - o Note: An exception is when there is reason to believe the patient or others are in severe, immediate danger to life or health
- When laws mandate a civil, criminal, or disciplinary action resulting from art therapy services. However, this should only be as reasonably necessary in that action's course.

THE EXCEPTIONS TO THE CLIENT'S RIGHT TO CONFIDENTIALITY IN THE THERAPY SETTING

It may be appropriate for the art therapist to consult with lawyers, a consultation agency, policy, or supervisors before releasing any confidential patient. Under the following situations, the art therapist may disclose confidential information:

- When the therapist believes it is in the patient's best interest and there is written consent from the patient or their legal guardian
- When law requires disclosure, such as when the patient is at risk for suicide, homicide, or child/elderly abuse or neglect
- When an ATCB disciplinary action requires disclosure but only as reasonably necessary in such cases
- When the art therapist is a defendant in a therapy-related civil criminal action

Use of Client Artwork

Release or Use of Patient Artwork Outside the Therapy Setting--Art therapists are required to obtain and maintain the patient or guardian's authorized consent for the release of the patient's art expression and other patient information on file, unless otherwise provided by state law in the state of practice.

Note: During a therapy session, the art therapist should not release a minor's confidential information obtained to their parent or guardian unless mandated or provided for by state law in the state of practice.

Artwork as a Clinical Document

Although art therapist's view the patient's artwork as the patient's own property, sound clinical practice necessitates documentation. The art expression created is considered documentation and part of the patient's clinical record. As such, it should be retained by the art therapist and/or agency or company for a reasonable amount of time, consistent with both state regulations and sound clinical best practice.

Releasing Artwork to a Client and/or Referral Therapist

Art therapists considered art expressions created during treatment session as patient property. Thus, it may be released to the patient or guardian at any time upon request during the treatment program and also upon termination. As the created art is also considered part of the patient's clinical record, copies of it will be kept in the patient's file. In these instances, the art therapist is required to notify the patient.

Art therapists are not to disclose confidential patient information for the consultation and supervision purposes without the patient's explicit consent, unless the therapist has reason to believe that the patient or others are in severe, immediate danger to life or health. Any such disclosure needs to be consistent with laws pertaining to the patient, family, and general public's welfare.

Displaying Patient Artwork

For either original or copies of the patient's artwork to be used for any means or in any way such as the following, the patient or their legal guardian must give written consent and sign release forms:

- Prior to photographing, video or audio taping, or otherwise duplicating or allowing third-party review or observation of a patient's art therapy sessions or produced works
- Before using in public presentations, teaching, or writing
- Before displaying the patient's artwork in galleries, schools, mental health facilities, or other public places and spaces

Additionally, the art therapist must always protect the patient's identity and artwork whenever it is used.

REFERRING A PATIENT

Therapy sometimes ends prematurely, before resolution of the problem. In such cases, the therapist may need to refer the patient to another professional. The following are some of the circumstances where the patient is referred to another health professional:

- When the therapist is unwilling or unable to continue providing professional help and support
- When the problem or indicated treatment is beyond the therapist's scope of practice, education, experience, and training
- For other appropriate reasons like avoiding a dual relationship or other conflict of interest

It would be an ethical violation to continue providing therapy in any of the above reasons.

QUALITY ASSURANCE

Quality assurance is a set of actions or system for evaluating performance, such as the delivery of therapeutic services to patients. Quality assurance is considered:

- An interdisciplinary profession or practice
- The responsibility of management personnel who are to plan and endure the quality of offered services

Quality assurance involves activities that provide needed evidence to instill confidence that the activities are being performed effectively and if quality to all those concerned. Quality assurance provides factually-based external confidence to patients and other stakeholders that provides services meet patient needs, expectations, and other such requirements. It assures the existence and effectiveness of procedures intended to assure that the expected quality levels will be achieved.

Quality assurance and quality control are often used interchangeably.

CONTINUOUS QUALITY IMPROVEMENT (CQI)

Continuous Quality Improvement is a broad term used in business management generally used to describe the systematic review and improving process of existing operational processes to best achieve the goal of patient satisfaction. It usually includes cost-effective high-quality services.

The following are some basic CQI concepts:

- Focus on the patient
- Eliminate all activities that do not add value to the quality providing process
- On-going or continual activities or processes that are linked together by groups of people or teams directed towards a common objective

MONITORING PATIENT CARE

In an institutional setting, to receive quality care, a patient must be able to access high-quality services that are produced consistently and evaluated and improved continually. It is the institution's responsibility to accomplish this through a Quality Assurance (QA) and an independent monitoring system, both which systematically review the processes, methods, and procedures used to reach mandated standards and goals. By identifying trends, strengths, and weaknesses program services offered to patients can be improved. These programs also must comply with the 1980 Mental Health Systems Act patient bill of rights.

MENTAL HEALTH SYSTEMS ACT

The patient has the following rights:

- The treatment should be provided in the least restrictive setting
- Their written treatment plan should be accurate and individualized and should include a discharge plan of care
- The right to participate in the treatment plan's construction and revision
- The right to obtain information about alternative treatment strategies and those treatments' possible beneficial and adverse effects
- The right to refuse treatment except in emergency situations or those defined by specific state laws in the state of practice
- The right not to have restraints or be secluded except in emergency situations
- The right to be placed in a humane treatment setting
- The right to confidentiality of their medical records
- The right to access their mental health records
- The right to conversations with others
- The right to access a telephone and mail
- The right to have visitors, unless restricted due to specific treatment plan stipulations
- The right to civil right information
- The right to advocate and receive assistance from others
- The right to refuse to participate in experiments or other research
- The right to declare grievances, which should be heard in a timely and fair manner

REPORTING ABUSE OR NEGLECT

There is a mandatory child and elderly neglect and abuse reporting law in each state in order for them to qualify for federal funding. The following are some included statutes:

- A hotline for people to report neglect and abuse
- Mandatory reporting for certain professionals (such as mental health providers, physicians, social workers, police officers, teachers and others who generally have frequent contact with either children or the elderly) and institutions to be able to report suspected abuse.
- Causes for reporting vary from a mere "reasonable suspicion" or "reasonable cause to believe" to "know or suspect."
- Legal consequences inflicted for failing to report
- Immunity from potential prosecution arising from reporting abuse or neglect. An individual who reports any suspected abuse in "good faith", in most states, is immune from all criminal and civil liability.
- Prosecution in cases of false reporting (reports made in the absence of having a reasonable belief)
- Reports are made to a law enforcement authority of some type or a protection agency.

TARASOFF DECISION

Because of the rulings in the California Supreme Court's decision in Tarasoff v. Regents of the University of California (17 Cal.3d 425 [1976]), all psychotherapists in the United States must handle patient threats carefully. The court decided that if a psychotherapist either determines or should have reasonably determined "that a patient poses a serious danger of violence to others, he bears a duty to exercise reasonable care to protect the foreseeable victim of that danger." Since then, two additional court cases have extended the Tarasoff decision's reach by including those threats reportedly made by a patient but later revealed to a psychotherapist by the patient's relative.

SUBPOENAS

Upon receipt of a subpoena, release of patient records can be complicated, because sometimes legal requirements conflict with copyright laws and ethical guidelines. Since the laws vary between states, it is advisable for psychotherapists to consult with an attorney in their own state. Typically, a therapist is expected to protect the patient's right to confidentiality, encouraged to notify patients when their records have been subpoenaed, and to confirm receipt of signed authorization-to-release-records form from patients before releasing any information. Although every state recognizes some therapist-patient privileges, under the Federal Rules of Evidence, the issue remains unresolved for the United States federal courts.

An art therapist's ability to protect the patient-therapist relationship are varied but may include the source, the welfare of the patient and others, state and federal laws, and ethical codes. Recent federal laws enacted, such as HIPAA (Health Insurance

Portability and Accountability Act), permit the release of patient records when subpoenaed without the patient's consent or knowledge. However, HIPAA contains a preemptive clause such that when HIPAA and state laws conflict, the more protective privacy law (HIPAA or state) applies. In general, state laws provide more protection than HIPAA. Therefore, preemption analysis usually indicate that test data or records cannot be released for a subpoena alone.

SPECIAL COURT SUBPOENAS

Any requested records may be subject to investigation and release with an FBI subpoenas and the patient may not receive notification.

When the therapist responds to a subpoena that is accompanied by the patient's signed authorization, he or she should continue to exert the utmost effort to protect the patient's confidentiality and welfare before releasing any information by following these procedures:

- Assert or document any concerns about the information release that could be damaging to the involved patient
- Offer to provide a record summary instead of the complete records on file
- Unless court ordered otherwise, release as little as possible
- If necessary, to release any confidential information about other people discussed in the therapy, exercise extreme caution

AMERICANS WITH DISABILITIES ACT

The Americans with Disabilities Act (ADA) (P.L. 101-336) is considered the most comprehensive civil rights legislation enacted to prohibit discrimination against individuals with disabilities. The law requires state and local government agencies, public and private businesses, private entities providing public services and accommodations, and utilities and transportation to comply. A disability is a mental or physical impairment that "limits one or more major life activities" for the individual. Major life activities include one's ability for self-care, learning, working, walking, seeing, hearing, speaking, breathing, or maintaining social relationships. Individuals with disabilities may receive various types of therapy to restore, improve, or develop impaired or lost functions. Therapy may target a range of functions (e.g., speech, ambulation, daily life activities, feeding) and may be of a variety of forms (e.g., dance, music or art therapy).

OLDER AMERICANS ACT

The Older Americans Act assists the development of programs targeted for older adults through state grants for community planning and services. The goal of the act is to secure an adequate standard of living in for older adults in retirement. The Older Americans Act, at the federal level, authorizes state grants to provide art therapy to older adults as a supportive service to enable them to attain and maintain healthy well-being. Art therapy, according to the act, is defined as the "use of art and artistic processes specifically selected and administered by an art therapist, to accomplish the restoration, maintenance, or improvement of the mental, emotional, or social functioning of an older individual."

UNIVERSAL PRECAUTIONS

The term "universal precautions" describes the practices of hygiene to follow when exposed to confirmed or potential disease-carrying bodily fluids such as the following:

- Blood or other body fluids visibly containing blood
- Semen and vaginal secretions and sexual fluids
- Tissues
- Cerebrospinal fluid (CSF), amniotic fluid, synovial fluid, pleural fluid, pericardial fluid, and peritoneal fluid

Universal precautions do not apply to the following bodily fluids:

- feces
- nasal secretions
- vomit (unless visible blood is contained)
- sputum
- sweat
- tears
- urine

The basic hygienic practices implicated by universal precautions are designed to protect anyone who may come in contact with potentially disease-containing body fluids. The word "universal" is used because the precautions offer protection against many germs that can causes disease.

The following are included under universal precautions:

- Barrier protection (i.e., disposable gloves, lab coats, and eye and face protection) should be used.
- Because specifying the requisite specific barrier types for every possible clinical situation would be impractical, it is prudent to exercise best judgment.
- Thorough and frequent washing of hands and wrists
- Handling all instruments cautiously

RESEARCH METHODOLOGIES

Researchers are subject to professional standards, laws, and regulations governing research conduct. Art therapists might employ the following research methodologies:

- Case history: a detailed factual account regarding a patient, group, or treatment's development or condition.
- Qualitative research: used to understand a patient's intentions, motivations, mind, feelings, and thoughts. Compared to quantitative research, qualitative is typically conducted with a smaller sample and is thus only partially representative of the population from which the sample is drawn. As such, this research cannot and should not be projected to the whole population, but is used to provide more general indications. Methods of qualitative research include focus group discussions and interviews.
- Quantitative research: conducted with larger samples and yields quantifiable results that can be statistically projected and meaningful to a larger population. Normal quantitative methods include interviews, surveys, and questionnaires.

QUANTITATIVE AND QUALITATIVE RESEARCH APPROACHES COMPARED:

Quantitative	Qualitative
Objective	Subjective
Deductive	Inductive
Generalizable	Not generalizable
Numbers	Words
Requires a hypothesis	Does not require a hypothesis

Both types use a systematic approach.

RESEARCH GUIDELINES

Art therapists conducting research must protect the welfare of their participants and respect their dignity. To do so, the art therapist should follow these guidelines:

- Seek qualified, independent professionals for advice regarding avoiding any potential ethical issues
- Provide thorough information about all aspects of the planned research that may influence participation decisions
- Allow participants to freely reject and/or withdraw their participation without incurring adverse consequences
- Obtain informed consent for participation of all participants or guardians, including those with limit decision-making abilities. Consent should also address the use and/or release of results or the participant's information obtained in the research
- Develop a sound plan to protect participants' confidentiality including any access by others

- Use an appropriate, culturally-competent interview style:
  - o Ask open-ended questions
  - o Conduct assessments empathetically
  - o Discover the patient's beliefs
  - o Use reflective listening

How to Overcome Test Anxiety

Just the thought of taking a test is enough to make most people a little nervous. A test is an important event that can have a long-term impact on your future, so it's important to take it seriously and it's natural to feel anxious about performing well. But just because anxiety is normal, that doesn't mean that it's helpful in test taking, or that you should simply accept it as part of your life. Anxiety can have a variety of effects. These effects can be mild, like making you feel slightly nervous, or severe, like blocking your ability to focus or remember even a simple detail.

If you experience test anxiety—whether severe or mild—it's important to know how to beat it. To discover this, first you need to understand what causes test anxiety.

Causes of Test Anxiety

While we often think of anxiety as an uncontrollable emotional state, it can actually be caused by simple, practical things. One of the most common causes of test anxiety is that a person does not feel adequately prepared for their test. This feeling can be the result of many different issues such as poor study habits or lack of organization, but the most common culprit is time management. Starting to study too late, failing to organize your study time to cover all of the material, or being distracted while you study will mean that you're not well prepared for the test. This may lead to cramming the night before, which will cause you to be physically and mentally exhausted for the test. Poor time management also contributes to feelings of stress, fear, and hopelessness as you realize you are not well prepared but don't know what to do about it.

Other times, test anxiety is not related to your preparation for the test but comes from unresolved fear. This may be a past failure on a test, or poor performance on tests in general. It may come from comparing yourself to others who seem to be performing better or from the stress of living up to expectations. Anxiety may be driven by fears of the future—how failure on this test would affect your educational and career goals. These fears are often completely irrational, but they can still negatively impact your test performance.

> **Review Video: <u>3 Reasons You Have Test Anxiety</u>**
> Visit mometrix.com/academy and enter code: 428468

Elements of Test Anxiety

As mentioned earlier, test anxiety is considered to be an emotional state, but it has physical and mental components as well. Sometimes you may not even realize that you are suffering from test anxiety until you notice the physical symptoms. These can include trembling hands, rapid heartbeat, sweating, nausea, and tense muscles. Extreme anxiety may lead to fainting or vomiting. Obviously, any of these symptoms can have a negative impact on testing. It is important to recognize them as soon as they begin to occur so that you can address the problem before it damages your performance.

> **Review Video: 3 Ways to Tell You Have Test Anxiety**
> Visit mometrix.com/academy and enter code: 927847

The mental components of test anxiety include trouble focusing and inability to remember learned information. During a test, your mind is on high alert, which can help you recall information and stay focused for an extended period of time. However, anxiety interferes with your mind's natural processes, causing you to blank out, even on the questions you know well. The strain of testing during anxiety makes it difficult to stay focused, especially on a test that may take several hours. Extreme anxiety can take a huge mental toll, making it difficult not only to recall test information but even to understand the test questions or pull your thoughts together.

> **Review Video: How Test Anxiety Affects Memory**
> Visit mometrix.com/academy and enter code: 609003

Effects of Test Anxiety

Test anxiety is like a disease—if left untreated, it will get progressively worse. Anxiety leads to poor performance, and this reinforces the feelings of fear and failure, which in turn lead to poor performances on subsequent tests. It can grow from a mild nervousness to a crippling condition. If allowed to progress, test anxiety can have a big impact on your schooling, and consequently on your future.

Test anxiety can spread to other parts of your life. Anxiety on tests can become anxiety in any stressful situation, and blanking on a test can turn into panicking in a job situation. But fortunately, you don't have to let anxiety rule your testing and determine your grades. There are a number of relatively simple steps you can take to move past anxiety and function normally on a test and in the rest of life.

> **Review Video: How Test Anxiety Impacts Your Grades**
> Visit mometrix.com/academy and enter code: 939819

Physical Steps for Beating Test Anxiety

While test anxiety is a serious problem, the good news is that it can be overcome. It doesn't have to control your ability to think and remember information. While it may take time, you can begin taking steps today to beat anxiety.

Just as your first hint that you may be struggling with anxiety comes from the physical symptoms, the first step to treating it is also physical. Rest is crucial for having a clear, strong mind. If you are tired, it is much easier to give in to anxiety. But if you establish good sleep habits, your body and mind will be ready to perform optimally, without the strain of exhaustion. Additionally, sleeping well helps you to retain information better, so you're more likely to recall the answers when you see the test questions.

Getting good sleep means more than going to bed on time. It's important to allow your brain time to relax. Take study breaks from time to time so it doesn't get overworked, and don't study right before bed. Take time to rest your mind before trying to rest your body, or you may find it difficult to fall asleep.

> **Review Video: <u>The Importance of Sleep for Your Brain</u>**
> Visit mometrix.com/academy and enter code: 319338

Along with sleep, other aspects of physical health are important in preparing for a test. Good nutrition is vital for good brain function. Sugary foods and drinks may give a burst of energy but this burst is followed by a crash, both physically and emotionally. Instead, fuel your body with protein and vitamin-rich foods.

Also, drink plenty of water. Dehydration can lead to headaches and exhaustion, especially if your brain is already under stress from the rigors of the test. Particularly if your test is a long one, drink water during the breaks. And if possible, take an energy-boosting snack to eat between sections.

> **Review Video: <u>How Diet Can Affect your Mood</u>**
> Visit mometrix.com/academy and enter code: 624317

Along with sleep and diet, a third important part of physical health is exercise. Maintaining a steady workout schedule is helpful, but even taking 5-minute study breaks to walk can help get your blood pumping faster and clear your head. Exercise also releases endorphins, which contribute to a positive feeling and can help combat test anxiety.

When you nurture your physical health, you are also contributing to your mental health. If your body is healthy, your mind is much more likely to be healthy as well. So take time to rest, nourish your body with healthy food and water, and get moving as much as possible. Taking these physical steps will make you stronger and more able to take the mental steps necessary to overcome test anxiety.

Mental Steps for Beating Test Anxiety

Working on the mental side of test anxiety can be more challenging, but as with the physical side, there are clear steps you can take to overcome it. As mentioned earlier, test anxiety often stems from lack of preparation, so the obvious solution is to prepare for the test. Effective studying may be the most important weapon you have for beating test anxiety, but you can and should employ several other mental tools to combat fear.

First, boost your confidence by reminding yourself of past success—tests or projects that you aced. If you're putting as much effort into preparing for this test as you did for those, there's no reason you should expect to fail here. Work hard to prepare; then trust your preparation.

Second, surround yourself with encouraging people. It can be helpful to find a study group, but be sure that the people you're around will encourage a positive attitude. If you spend time with others who are anxious or cynical, this will only contribute to your own anxiety. Look for others who are motivated to study hard from a desire to succeed, not from a fear of failure.

Third, reward yourself. A test is physically and mentally tiring, even without anxiety, and it can be helpful to have something to look forward to. Plan an activity following the test, regardless of the outcome, such as going to a movie or getting ice cream.

When you are taking the test, if you find yourself beginning to feel anxious, remind yourself that you know the material. Visualize successfully completing the test. Then take a few deep, relaxing breaths and return to it. Work through the questions carefully but with confidence, knowing that you are capable of succeeding.

Developing a healthy mental approach to test taking will also aid in other areas of life. Test anxiety affects more than just the actual test—it can be damaging to your mental health and even contribute to depression. It's important to beat test anxiety before it becomes a problem for more than testing.

Review Video: Test Anxiety and Depression
Visit mometrix.com/academy and enter code: 904704

Study Strategy

Being prepared for the test is necessary to combat anxiety, but what does being prepared look like? You may study for hours on end and still not feel prepared. What you need is a strategy for test prep. The next few pages outline our recommended steps to help you plan out and conquer the challenge of preparation.

STEP 1: SCOPE OUT THE TEST

Learn everything you can about the format (multiple choice, essay, etc.) and what will be on the test. Gather any study materials, course outlines, or sample exams that may be available. Not only will this help you to prepare, but knowing what to expect can help to alleviate test anxiety.

STEP 2: MAP OUT THE MATERIAL

Look through the textbook or study guide and make note of how many chapters or sections it has. Then divide these over the time you have. For example, if a book has 15 chapters and you have five days to study, you need to cover three chapters each day. Even better, if you have the time, leave an extra day at the end for overall review after you have gone through the material in depth.

If time is limited, you may need to prioritize the material. Look through it and make note of which sections you think you already have a good grasp on, and which need review. While you are studying, skim quickly through the familiar sections and take more time on the challenging parts. Write out your plan so you don't get lost as you go. Having a written plan also helps you feel more in control of the study, so anxiety is less likely to arise from feeling overwhelmed at the amount to cover.

STEP 3: GATHER YOUR TOOLS

Decide what study method works best for you. Do you prefer to highlight in the book as you study and then go back over the highlighted portions? Or do you type out notes of the important information? Or is it helpful to make flashcards that you can carry with you? Assemble the pens, index cards, highlighters, post-it notes, and any other materials you may need so you won't be distracted by getting up to find things while you study.

If you're having a hard time retaining the information or organizing your notes, experiment with different methods. For example, try color-coding by subject with colored pens, highlighters, or post-it notes. If you learn better by hearing, try recording yourself reading your notes so you can listen while in the car, working out, or simply sitting at your desk. Ask a friend to quiz you from your flashcards, or try teaching someone the material to solidify it in your mind.

STEP 4: CREATE YOUR ENVIRONMENT

It's important to avoid distractions while you study. This includes both the obvious distractions like visitors and the subtle distractions like an uncomfortable chair (or a too-comfortable couch that makes you want to fall asleep). Set up the best study environment possible: good lighting and a comfortable work area. If background music helps you focus, you may want to turn it on, but otherwise keep the room quiet. If you are using a computer to take notes, be sure you don't have any other windows open, especially applications like social media, games, or anything else that could distract you. Silence your phone and turn off notifications. Be sure to keep water close by so you stay hydrated while you study (but avoid unhealthy drinks and snacks).

Also, take into account the best time of day to study. Are you freshest first thing in the morning? Try to set aside some time then to work through the material. Is your mind clearer in the afternoon or evening? Schedule your study session then. Another method is to study at the same time of day that you will take the test, so that your brain gets used to working on the material at that time and will be ready to focus at test time.

STEP 5: STUDY!

Once you have done all the study preparation, it's time to settle into the actual studying. Sit down, take a few moments to settle your mind so you can focus, and begin to follow your study plan. Don't give in to distractions or let yourself procrastinate. This is your time to prepare so you'll be ready to fearlessly approach the test. Make the most of the time and stay focused.

Of course, you don't want to burn out. If you study too long you may find that you're not retaining the information very well. Take regular study breaks. For example, taking five minutes out of every hour to walk briskly, breathing deeply and swinging your arms, can help your mind stay fresh.

As you get to the end of each chapter or section, it's a good idea to do a quick review. Remind yourself of what you learned and work on any difficult parts. When you feel that you've mastered the material, move on to the next part. At the end of your study session, briefly skim through your notes again.

But while review is helpful, cramming last minute is NOT. If at all possible, work ahead so that you won't need to fit all your study into the last day. Cramming overloads your brain with more information than it can process and retain, and your tired mind may struggle to recall even previously learned information when it is overwhelmed with last-minute study. Also, the urgent nature of cramming and the stress placed on your brain contribute to anxiety. You'll be more likely to go to the test feeling unprepared and having trouble thinking clearly.

So don't cram, and don't stay up late before the test, even just to review your notes at a leisurely pace. Your brain needs rest more than it needs to go over the information again. In fact, plan to finish your studies by noon or early afternoon the day before the test. Give your brain the rest of the day to relax or focus on other things, and get a good night's sleep. Then you will be fresh for the test and better able to recall what you've studied.

STEP 6: TAKE A PRACTICE TEST

Many courses offer sample tests, either online or in the study materials. This is an excellent resource to check whether you have mastered the material, as well as to prepare for the test format and environment.

Check the test format ahead of time: the number of questions, the type (multiple choice, free response, etc.), and the time limit. Then create a plan for working through them. For example, if you have 30 minutes to take a 60-question test, your limit is 30 seconds per question. Spend less time on the questions you know well so that you can take more time on the difficult ones.

If you have time to take several practice tests, take the first one open book, with no time limit. Work through the questions at your own pace and make sure you fully understand them. Gradually work up to taking a test under test conditions: sit at a desk with all study materials put away and set a timer. Pace yourself to make sure you finish the test with time to spare and go back to check your answers if you have time.

After each test, check your answers. On the questions you missed, be sure you understand why you missed them. Did you misread the question (tests can use tricky wording)? Did you forget the information? Or was it something you hadn't learned? Go back and study any shaky areas that the practice tests reveal.

Taking these tests not only helps with your grade, but also aids in combating test anxiety. If you're already used to the test conditions, you're less likely to worry about it, and working through tests until you're scoring well gives you a confidence boost. Go through the practice tests until you feel comfortable, and then you can go into the test knowing that you're ready for it.

Test Tips

On test day, you should be confident, knowing that you've prepared well and are ready to answer the questions. But aside from preparation, there are several test day strategies you can employ to maximize your performance.

First, as stated before, get a good night's sleep the night before the test (and for several nights before that, if possible). Go into the test with a fresh, alert mind rather than staying up late to study.

Try not to change too much about your normal routine on the day of the test. It's important to eat a nutritious breakfast, but if you normally don't eat breakfast at all, consider eating just a protein bar. If you're a coffee drinker, go ahead and have your normal coffee. Just make sure you time it so that the caffeine doesn't wear off right in the middle of your test. Avoid sugary beverages, and drink enough water to stay hydrated but not so much that you need a restroom break 10 minutes into the test. If your test isn't first thing in the morning, consider going for a walk or doing a light workout before the test to get your blood flowing.

Allow yourself enough time to get ready, and leave for the test with plenty of time to spare so you won't have the anxiety of scrambling to arrive in time. Another reason to be early is to select a good seat. It's helpful to sit away from doors and windows, which can be distracting. Find a good seat, get out your supplies, and settle your mind before the test begins.

When the test begins, start by going over the instructions carefully, even if you already know what to expect. Make sure you avoid any careless mistakes by following the directions.

Then begin working through the questions, pacing yourself as you've practiced. If you're not sure on an answer, don't spend too much time on it, and don't let it shake your confidence. Either skip it and come back later, or eliminate as many wrong answers as possible and guess among the remaining ones. Don't dwell on these questions as you continue—put them out of your mind and focus on what lies ahead.

Be sure to read all of the answer choices, even if you're sure the first one is the right answer. Sometimes you'll find a better one if you keep reading. But don't second-guess yourself if you do immediately know the answer. Your gut instinct is usually right. Don't let test anxiety rob you of the information you know.

If you have time at the end of the test (and if the test format allows), go back and review your answers. Be cautious about changing any, since your first instinct tends to be correct, but make sure you didn't misread any of the questions or accidentally mark the wrong answer choice. Look over any you skipped and make an educated guess.

At the end, leave the test feeling confident. You've done your best, so don't waste time worrying about your performance or wishing you could change anything. Instead, celebrate the successful completion of this test. And finally, use this test to learn how to deal with anxiety even better next time.

> **Review Video: 5 Tips to Beat Test Anxiety**
> Visit mometrix.com/academy and enter code: 570656

Important Qualification

Not all anxiety is created equal. If your test anxiety is causing major issues in your life beyond the classroom or testing center, or if you are experiencing troubling physical symptoms related to your anxiety, it may be a sign of a serious physiological or psychological condition. If this sounds like your situation, we strongly encourage you to seek professional help.

Thank You

We at Mometrix would like to extend our heartfelt thanks to you, our friend and patron, for allowing us to play a part in your journey. It is a privilege to serve people from all walks of life who are unified in their commitment to building the best future they can for themselves.

The preparation you devote to these important testing milestones may be the most valuable educational opportunity you have for making a real difference in your life. We encourage you to put your heart into it—that feeling of succeeding, overcoming, and yes, conquering will be well worth the hours you've invested.

We want to hear your story, your struggles and your successes, and if you see any opportunities for us to improve our materials so we can help others even more effectively in the future, please share that with us as well. **The team at Mometrix would be absolutely thrilled to hear from you!** So please, send us an email (support@mometrix.com) and let's stay in touch.

> **If you'd like some additional help, check out these other resources we offer for your exam:**
> **http://mometrixflashcards.com/ArtTherapy**

Additional Bonus Material

Due to our efforts to try to keep this book to a manageable length, we've created a link that will give you access to all of your additional bonus material:

<u>mometrix.com/bonus948/arttherapy</u>